MW00618386

PRO-CHOICE
PRO-ADOPTION

PRO-CHOICE PRO-ADOPTION

It's Time for a Loving, Positive Response
to Unplanned Pregnancy

THERESA (TERRI) MARCROFT

GLOBAL PRESS OF SILICON VALLEY

ISBN: 978-1-7357534-6-1 (Paperback)
ISBN: 978-1-7357534-5-4 (E-book)

Library of Congress Control Number: 2022919773

GLOBAL PRESS OF SILICON VALLEY,
P.O. Box 28153, San Jose, CA 95129-8153

To my daughter, Sydney.
Being your mom has been the joy—and the purpose—of my life.

To her birth mother.
We are both grateful, beyond words, for the choices you made.

Early Praise for
Pro-Choice, Pro-Adoption.
It's Time for a Loving, Positive Response to Unplanned Pregnancy

"This book reminds us that fathers and partners need to advocate for the women they love—especially when they face an unplanned pregnancy. Open adoption is a loving, positive response worth careful consideration."
— Matt Birk, Super Bowl champion,
pro-life advocate, and father of eight

This book is a refreshing and hopeful look at adoption. The author does an excellent job of exposing the old, unhealthy paradigms of closed adoption, and brings forth the beauty and possibility that adoption can hold for a woman who is not ready to parent. She can be empowered to choose parents to raise her child, and through open adoption, keep contact and communication open with the child and the adoptive family."
— Valerie Hill Experienced teen mom, post abortive mom,
and stepmom to an adopted son CEO, RealOptions Medical Clinics

"This book provides wonderful and unique insight into exactly what we as a country, as a culture, as a faith community, and as a family need to hear. We can, and must, do better to advocate for open adoption."
— Tim Elder Founder of InfantAdoptionGuide.com
and dad of three through adoption

"Being pro-choice means supporting women in all of their options, including adoption. In some cases, making an adoption plan is the best choice."
— Kelly Perey, Management & career coach,
retired Silicon Valley executive, pro-choice, mother of four

"What I loved about this book are the many first-hand testimonies that reflect the true birth parent experience. The transparency of the stories is soul stirring!"

— Courtney Tierra Author, proud speaker on the
birth mom experience www.courtneytierra.com/

"This book makes an important point: Supporting adoption is good for business, in the short and long term, because it's better for women's health."

— Peter Rex
Founder/CEO, Rex

"Theresa Marcroft brings her true love and concern for all three persons in the "adoption triad" to this important book. As an adoptive mom herself, Theresa has devoted the last decade of her life to advocating for more transparency and education around adoption. This book, Pro-Choice, Pro-Adoption. It's Time for a Loving, Positive Response to Unplanned Pregnancy, is full of illuminating facts about the current practice of adoption in the U.S., and is a must-read for any practitioner, adoptive parent, or birth parent. Adoptees will also benefit from her passionate focus on giving voice to the complex realities of these relationships. If you are touched by adoption in any way, or considering getting involved, this book is a rare find that will guide you with light and love."

— Jodi Jackson Tucker
President, Second Mothers,
www.secondmothers.org

"I worked with teenagers as a teacher, head coach, and keynote speaker for over 20 years. Many young people have good intentions but lack the life experience to navigate the unexpected. Young adults often choose the quickest solution to a problem without grasping the long-term consequences, especially if doing so helps them avoid angering or disappointing their parents. Those young people really need guidance, and this book offers a new perspective to those who advise them. The case studies give a glimpse into the stories of others who faced unintended pregnancies and how healthy open adoption can be for all involved. I highly recommend this book."

— Tom Gose
https://www.tomgose.com/

Table of Contents

Foreword:
One Birth Mother's Thoughts

Things like this don't happen to people like me and my family.

I remember thinking to myself, "When could this possibly have happened? And how could this possibly have happened? I don't even have a 'bump.' This has got to be a mistake." Six positive pregnancy tests later, I was finally convinced this baby was, indeed, really happening.

After my 24-hour pity party, I called my older sister, Claire. I had every intention of telling her about my pregnancy, but once we started talking, I couldn't find it in myself to utter the words, "I'm pregnant." Through my uncontrollable sobbing, I managed to tell her, "I just need to get away." She told me to come stay with her for a while.

I loaded my car with personal belongings necessary for the next three months and got on the road. I remember pulling over at a gas station thirty minutes away from my sister's house and writing her a letter explaining the real reason I needed to get out of my hometown. The judgments, the local chatter, and the people who would feel the need to insert themselves and their opinions in a situation they knew nothing about—I refused to subject myself to all that. She would understand.

When I arrived and handed her the letter, she read it, calmly folded it back up, and without any judgment in her voice said, "OK, what's your next step, and what can I do to help?" My family is more than capable of supporting me financially, mentally, and emotionally, but this was my decision. I told Claire the only option that came to my mind was to place my child for adoption. Our family has been fortunate enough to have three beautiful blessings in our lives, thanks to brave women who made the decision to place their children.

The next day, Claire contacted an organization here in Kentucky—the one I later chose to place my child. From the second they answered the phone, their focus was on me and my child. Our case worker, Rita, offered to drive to Claire's house to make our first meeting as comfortable and easy as possible. With Rita, we discussed my different adoption options. I told her I was 100% positive I wanted a closed adoption: I just wanted to get through the pregnancy, move forward, and forget about this entire chapter of my life. Rita gave me the names of local doctors. Given how far I was along in my pregnancy, she advised me to get in as soon as I could. Unfortunately, the earliest appointment I could get anywhere was a month down the road. That was one of the longest months of my life.

When the appointment day finally arrived, the nurse asked me how far along I thought I was, and I told her "Oh, I think about 7 months or so. . . ." She chuckled as she took a step back and looked at me again saying, "I don't think so, but we'll see once the doctor gets you on the table and we do your ultrasound."

> **"The ultrasound changed my mind about having a closed adoption. Once I saw her, I knew I only wanted an open adoption."**

That ultrasound forever changed my life. I remember the tech saying, "It's a girl, and oh my goodness, look at all that hair!" I just stared at her with eyes swollen with tears and my heart the fullest it has ever been. Claire and I laughed about how cute she was with my lips and chubby cheeks. She was adorable, even in pixilated black and white.

That ultrasound didn't change my decision to place her for adoption, but it did change my mind about having a closed adoption. As soon as I saw her, I immediately knew there was no way I could go on with my life without seeing her again. Now I only wanted an open adoption.

When I called Rita, she said she would bring profiles of couples looking for open adoptions who fit within the criteria that I wanted. A few days later, Claire and I carefully reviewed the profiles. I just didn't have that "Yes—this is the couple" feeling. Four different cities and almost thirty couple profiles later, I still wasn't any closer to finding THE one. It was less than a month before my due date. I worried if I'd ever find the perfect couple to raise my beautiful baby girl. Rita and Claire assured me they were out there: "We'll go all the way to California if we have to, in order to find a couple you're comfortable raising your child."

Finally. Seeing Shawn & Cheryl's profile was a moment in my life I'll never forget. We had the same likes and dislikes. Their values, morals, and lifestyles were exactly what I was looking to find. For the first time since finding out I was pregnant, I was excited. They were just like me. I wanted to meet them immediately.

Rita coordinated with Shawn & Cheryl's case worker to arrange a meeting. Claire and I were both a nervous wreck. *Would they like me? Will they be just as perfect in person as they were on paper? Will they really allow me to see her after she is born? Will they allow her to have a relationship with her birth father as well? (Even though I had zero relationship with him, this was important to me.) What if we just don't have that connection?* While walking in, I prayed, "Please just show me a sign that they are the couple for my baby."

> ## I didn't "lose" Olivia. I gained three of the most beautiful people.

The meeting began, and they were even better than I could have ever imagined. At one point, I was reviewing my reasons for choosing adoption and I mentioned how two of my cousins had adopted a beautiful baby girl. I went on to say their names and Shawn & Cheryl's case worker apologetically stopped me and asked my cousins' full names. I told her and she said, "Oh my gosh. I was their case worker! I placed that beautiful little cousin you are talking about with them!" Claire and I immediately began crying. That was the sign we had prayed for. I knew right then that I wanted to place my baby girl with Shawn & Cheryl.

This was it. Here is my family to go through this amazing journey with together.

Our healthy, beautiful, and perfect little girl, Olivia, came into the world on February 7th, 2013. A special date not only because it's the day all of our lives changed, but because she shares a birthday with one of our family members who was adopted.

Our hospital stay was unique. What could have been such a sterile and sad time was replaced with a pizza party, a champagne toast, and Olivia being surrounded by an enormous amount of love from both my family and Shawn & Cheryl.

All of us were emotionally drained when it was time to leave the hospital. The closeness that had developed in our version of a modern family was something I've never experienced before, and doubt I ever will again. People see that we share family vacations and holidays together, and they have a hard time understanding our family dynamic. They think we are too close, or that we're only setting ourselves up for a tough road ahead once Olivia gets older. In the beginning, we had a very open and honest conversation establishing healthy boundaries. Two things were always at the forefront of those discussions: Olivia's best interests and Olivia always feeling the massive amount of love for her in this large, extended family. That's all any parent would want for their child. Shawn and Cheryl are the perfect couple to parent Olivia.

I didn't "lose" Olivia. If anything, I gained three of the most beautiful people, inside and out. I am so grateful to have them in my life. They have become two of the people with whom I want to share my happiest news and who I lean on for support during more trying times. I love how much we all have in common. Whether it's music, food, our loves of family, healthy lifestyles, or moral values—we've always seen eye-to-eye.

When Cheryl and I are out together, people ask if she is my sister. We always say "yes," because we are soul sisters. We just *get* each other. I feel like we've known each other for years. Cheryl has become one of the most important people in my life. My relationship with Shawn is one that keeps me laughing, and that I wouldn't change for anything. His sense of humor and love of life and family have had such a positive impact on my life. Every time I watch Shawn and Cheryl with Olivia, I'm reminded of how blessed my family and I are to have them in our lives.

There is not one single thing that I would have changed about my adoption journey. I had zero sadness or regret associated with my decision. Sometimes I do feel guilty or wrong for not feeling those ways, but I truly believe that if you're faced with a difficult decision and you know you're truly making the right choice, it's so much easier to make.

Not only did my family grow, but I grew as a person as well. Reflecting on my adoption journey, I feel more blessed than I ever imagined feeling at this point. I'm grateful for Rita for going above and beyond to match me with Shawn & Cheryl. I'm grateful for the relationships I have with Shawn & Cheryl, and the relationship they wanted me to have and allow me to have with Olivia. I'm grateful that my pregnancy and adoption journey has grown my family to include Shawn, Cheryl, & Olivia, and has also brought us so close.

"Grateful" is a perfect word to describe how I feel every single night when I lay down and realize all my adoption journey has given me.

– Ali Marie Watson

Preface:
Why This Matters to Me

The first "birth mother" I ever met was the one who chose my husband and me to parent her baby.

She was a high school student who had gotten pregnant in the middle of her senior year. By Spring, she was looking at stacks of profiles from hopeful, adoptive couples. My first conversation with "D" was on my 41st birthday. Since my husband was traveling on business, that first interaction was just the two of us.

It had already been a long journey. It seemed like we'd been struggling with infertility and working with adoption agencies forever. In truth, it was only about three years. Our first agency folded. The second one looked more promising. They called me to say that a young woman wanted to speak with us.

In our first conversation, which lasted about two hours, D said she was sure we were the right couple. We had met all of her criteria—the most unique one being that her child would have lots of cousins. My six siblings already had 14 kids, so that was a built-in tribe of cousins right there. Our first call ended with a plan to meet D and her mom for breakfast a few days later, when my husband could make the trip with me.

D had informed her mom that she was going to make an adoption plan. Her mom was on board with it, supportive. D had been planning on college and career, so both she and her mom quickly realized that becoming a parent in the summer after high school was not what they had hoped for her.

We drove the two hours north of San Jose, California to meet D in a Denny's on a Friday morning in early May, 1999. The four of us gathered for breakfast—D and her mom, my husband and me. It was the kind of breakfast conversation where the food is just a convenient coverup to mask the angst, apprehension, and anticipation we all felt. Nevertheless, that conversation over bagels was the first step in the merging of our four lives.

D had suggested the timing and location of that initial meeting so that we could go from there to her first ultrasound appointment.

We got to meet Sydney for the first time in 2D black & white. The ultrasound tech asked, "Do you want to know the sex?" D had told us she was sure she was carrying a boy. I can't remember who answered the technician's question, but yes, we were happy for any information we could get.

"It's a girl!" the tech continued, as she captured photo after photo, printing out two copies of each image. "One for your file, and one for you, D," the technician explained. Without missing a beat, D accepted the photos with one hand, then passed them over her belly to her other hand. She leaned in my direction, extending her arm, offering me the paper strip, "These are for you, Terri."

> **That was our first day together. Her openness would be the hallmark of our relationship in the coming months.**

D kept us informed and updated. She allowed my husband and me to participate in her pregnancy. I drove up to her town weekly to take her to lunch or join her for a doctor appointment. My husband accompanied me on these trips when he could. At D's suggestion, we made tapes of our voices, talking to the baby we hadn't yet met. She played the tapes to her belly, so that her baby could get familiar with our voices. In July, the three of us started Lamaze classes together, in preparation for her late August due date.

When Sydney was born, we were there at her birth to welcome her into the world. I'll forever be grateful that D was so open with us. Until I met her, I had been grieving my inability to bear a child, and somehow being able to participate in a few aspects of this pregnancy helped me with that.

That first night in the hospital, we took Sydney into D's room to say goodnight, and D asked if she could keep Sydney with her that night. My silent hesitation told her that I didn't think it was a good idea, to which D replied, "Terri, let Sydney stay with me this one night. You can have the next eighteen years with her."

And that began a life-long habit of answering yes to this woman—every time, without fail.

Keep in touch? Yes.

Send photos every two months, at least? Definitely.

Make sure she gets to know her cousins? Absolutely.

These promises were made the next day, through streams of tears. The four of us stood in the hospital foyer, sobbing as we struggled to find the words before taking Sydney home. It was a bittersweet goodbye.

Our debt to D is unrepayable. (If that's not a word, it should be.)

During the next few years, Sydney's birth mom was busy with college, and healing. After graduating, D decided to join the military. She contacted me to say she was enlisting and would soon leave for Officer Training School, after which she would request to be stationed in Iraq. In case she didn't return, she explained, she wanted to visit us for a weekend. Sydney was in kindergarten at that time. Although we didn't provide a lot of details, this was the first reunion for the four of us since that tear-filled day we left the hospital.

Sydney's early years in elementary school were unremarkable, busy, blessed—filled with homework, soccer, and chocolate. Her birth mom visited us when she came through California to see her own mom, but that was not often due to her work. When Sydney was about eleven years old, her birth mom settled down after six years of international travel with her job. That was also about the time that Sydney started asking more questions and showing more interest in her story. With each question, I shared more details, and usually stopped only when she lost interest in the conversation or changed the subject.

It's amazing how kids ask questions when they are ready to hear the answers.[1]

Our policy of total honesty served us both well. When all the dots connected in her mind—I could actually "see" the wheels turning—Sydney exclaimed, "OOOHHH!! THAT'S why you love D so much! SHE is the one who carried me!!" And it all fell into place for her.

At the same time, some of my own friends had delayed pregnancy, and faced infertility in their 40s. They tried to adopt but were unsuccessful. I didn't understand what the issue was and started on a mission to learn more. In Northern California, there were so very few women choosing adoption. Turns out that many young pregnant women aren't thinking about adoption, and the parents/mentors/teachers/pastors in their lives aren't suggesting it. As a result, there were (and still are) very few infants in need of a permanent family.

It broke my heart that my friends had unknowingly sacrificed their chance at motherhood. It was so sad that they were infertile and unable to adopt because only a tiny fraction of women facing unplanned pregnancy were choosing adoption. My dearest friends would never know the joy of a child's

---

1 If your child doesn't ask, though, you might test the waters by sharing a bit. Most are curious about their own story. And there are several good books on how to broach this subject, such as We Can Talk About It : A Conversation Starter for Foster and Adoptive Families by Whitney Bunker and Jena Holliday.

spontaneous hugs and kisses. They wouldn't know the reward of seeing their child make a wise decision or excel at something. They wouldn't know the satisfaction of seeing their child walk across a stage to accept a diploma. They wouldn't have a family.

That's when it became my passion to spread the word about open adoption. In 2010, I started a nonprofit organization, Unplanned Good, to do just that.

A few years later, when Sydney was 16, her birth mom contacted me again to ask us to come to her promotion ceremony in Hawaii. (Answer: Yes) We were preparing for this trip and talking about D when a lightbulb went off for Sydney. D was 16 when she got pregnant and made the decision to place her baby girl with us. Sydney was 16 when we traveled to D's promotion ceremony. Connecting those two things caused Sydney's eyes to suddenly grow huge: "MOM! NO WONDER she chose adoption! I mean, all I care about right now is soccer with my friends! No way could I be a mom!"

Sydney understood. She really "got" it. And we had come full circle. My daughter was perfectly clear on her whole story. And it's truly a thing of beauty.

Sydney has always seen us as her parents, day in and day out. And no additional information confused her in the slightest; it only added to her story. Honesty has always been a cornerstone of our relationship. Sydney can trust that she gets the truth from me. That approach has proven useful in so many areas of life and parenting. And, in hindsight, I can see that it paved the way for the close, healthy relationship we have today.

> ### *Honesty paves the way for a close, healthy relationship.*

The time is right to increase the volume on this option. The overturning of the Roe v Wade decision in 2022 brought the topic of unplanned pregnancy and our response to it to the forefront of discussions across the country. This is often presented as an "either-or" decision, suggesting that women must choose between abortion or parenting. Few are offering alternative solutions.

Even post-Roe, surprisingly, adoption is not on the radar when women evaluate their options. When a young woman faces the shock of an unplanned pregnancy, she turns most often to either her mom or to her male partner. But neither is suggesting adoption.

Why not?

This is what we want to dive into here.

If you'll bear with me as we review the current situation of unplanned pregnancy in the US, then I'll share with you the startling story of how much adoption has changed in the last few decades. The typical American doesn't know much about adoption and would be surprised to learn how it works today. We'll look at individuals and families who have been impacted by these birth mothers' decisions. You'll hear first-hand testimonials and real-life stories. Then we'll outline how we can bring about a cultural change in the way we respond to unplanned pregnancy in the US.

And WHY we will want to do just that.

—Terri Marcroft

PART ONE

PREGNANCY & ADOPTION IN THE US

Breaking Records in the USA

"Do the best you can until you know better. Then when you know better, do better."

— Maya Angelou

Section 1: The US is a Leader in Unplanned Pregnancy

In the last five years, the spotlight on the pro-life/pro-choice debate has intensified. In 2022, the Supreme Court reversed its 1973 decision on Roe v Wade, returning abortion policy decision-making to the states. With this ruling, the topic has become even more highly politicized. At its core, the root cause of this painful cultural divide is unplanned pregnancy.[2]

Here's where we are in 2022: Unplanned pregnancy is common in the US, very common.

Nearly half (45%) or 2.8 million of the 6.1 million pregnancies in the United States each year are unintended.[3] Rates of unintended pregnancy are higher among lower-income younger women between the ages of 18–24, cohabiting women, and minority women. Rates tend to be lower among higher-income women, white women, college graduates, and married women.[4]

---

2 Note: In this book, the phrases "unplanned pregnancy" and "unintended pregnancy" are used interchangeably.
3 https://www.guttmacher.org/fact-sheet/unintended-pregnancy-united-states
4 https://www.guttmacher.org/fact-sheet/unintended-pregnancy-united-states

The unintended pregnancy rate in the United States is higher than other developed countries, significantly higher than most—despite the widespread availability of birth control resources.

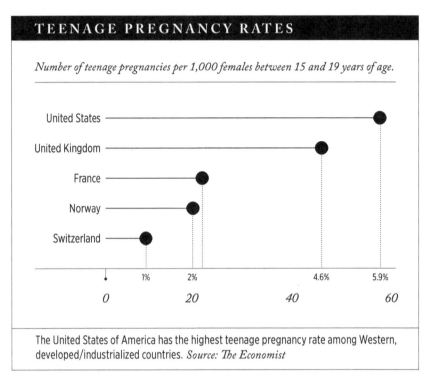

The United States of America has the highest teenage pregnancy rate among Western, developed/industrialized countries. *Source: The Economist*

The same is true for younger women: Teen pregnancy rates in the U.S. are also among the highest of industrialized nations.[5] In Switzerland, less than ten out of every 1,000 females between the ages of 15 and 19 become pregnant. In France and Norway, it's a little over 20 out every 1,000. England is higher, around 46 out of 1,000.[6] That's 1%, 2%, and 4.6% respectively. Currently, of all developed countries, America is the highest. Almost 60 out every 1,000 teens in the US, 6%, become pregnant before they reach 20 years old.[7]

---

5 The high rates of teen pregnancy are well-documented up to about 2016-2017. After that, government-published reports claim that teen pregnancy is decreasing but then support those with articles and figures on teen births. So we cannot be sure if teen pregnancies are decreasing at all, but rather suspect that any shift is due to the increase in teen abortions, which leads to fewer births by teen moms.

6 http://pregnancyadoptionoptions.com/why-americas-unplanned-pregnancy-rate-so-high/

7 http://pregnancyadoptionoptions.com/why-americas-unplanned-pregnancy-rate-so-high/

> ## *The US has the highest rate of teen pregnancy, and unplanned pregnancies in general, among economically-developed Western countries.*

The teenage pregnancy rate is strikingly higher in America than in most other prosperous countries, as are unplanned pregnancies in general. Over half of American conceptions are accidental, compared with a third in France.[8]

Consider the cumulative effect of these annual numbers to see the overall impact on our youth. Roughly 1 in 4 teen girls (25%) in the US gets pregnant at least once by age 20.[9] And about 1-in-6 teen births is a repeat birth.[10]

Section 2: The American Response to Unplanned Pregnancy

So, what becomes of all these unplanned pregnancies? The overwhelming majority of women in the US today believe they have only two choices when they face an unintended pregnancy–abortion or (often single) parenting. We see evidence of this, in that we lead the world in both categories.

The US abortion rate is among the highest of all Western countries.[11]

In 1991, the number of US abortions peaked at over 1.5 million. Through the 1990s and the 2000s, abortion decreased each year until around 2015, when the trend reversed direction. A marked increase was evident in each of the last six years. By 2020, abortion numbers were back up to 930,160 reported abortions. By 2022, the US ranked the 15th highest abortion rate among 57 countries tracked. The only "developed" countries with higher abortion rates than the USA were Estonia, Romania, Latvia, Hungary and Bulgaria.[12] The US has the highest abortion rate among the 'G7' most developed/industrialized countries in the world.[13]

---

8 https://www.economist.com/leaders/2015/04/18/dont-recoil-from-the-coil
9 Fast Facts: Teen Pregnancy in the United States | Power to Decide https://powertodecide.org/what-we-do/information/resource-library/fast-facts-teen-pregnancy-united-states
10 https://www.ncsl.org/research/health/teen-pregnancy-prevention.aspx and https://opa.hhs.gov/adolescent-health?adolescent-development/reproductive-health-and-teen-pregnancy/teen-pregnancy-and-childbearing/trends/index.html
11 https://worldpopulationreview.com/country-rankings/abortion-rates-by-country
12 Per the UN's Country Classification at un.org: World Economic Situation and Prospects 2014
13 IBID.

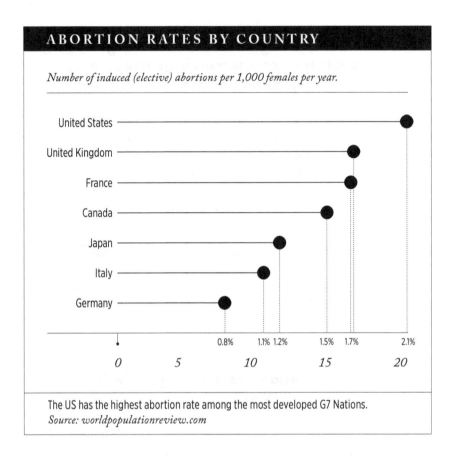

ABORTION RATES BY COUNTRY

Number of induced (elective) abortions per 1,000 females per year.

The US has the highest abortion rate among the most developed G7 Nations.
Source: worldpopulationreview.com

Historically, both unintended pregnancy rates and abortion rates are, on average, lower in high-income countries where people have greater access to family planning resources and education,[14] making it even more surprising that the US ranks so high on both measures.

---

14 Both unintended pregnancy rates and abortion rates are lower, on average, in high-income countries in which legal abortion is broadly available than in high-income countries with restrictive laws as well, as compared with low/middle-income countries regardless of the legal status of abortion. Some of this difference likely reflects greater access to family planning. https://gh.bmj.com/content/7/3/e007151

The USA also has the world's highest rate of children living in single-parent households.[15]

Unmarried women are choosing to parent at increasing rates. The share of U.S. children living with a single parent has been rising: In 1960, only 5% of moms were not married, but by 2015 that was 41%.[16] Each year, more single people become parents. This statistic goes hand-in-hand with a decline in marriage rates and a rise in births outside of marriage.[17]

SINGLE-PARENT HOUSEHOLDS			
US single-parenting households between 1960 and 2015.		*Globally, children under age 18 in single-parenting households.*	
2015	41%	United States	23%
2000	33%	United Kingdom	21%
1980	18%	Russia	18%
1960	5%	France	16%
		Brazil	10%
		Mexico	7%
		Turkey	2%
Incidents of US women parenting solo are on the rise. *Source: National Vital Statistics*		US children are more likely to live with a solo parent than any other nation. *Source: Pew Research Center*	

According to the US Census Bureau in April 2021, a single mother living with her child or children is the second most common living arrangement in the United States—a number that has doubled in the past 50 years.[18] As

---

15 https://www.pewresearch.org/fact-tank/2019/12/12/u-s-children-more-likely-than-children-in-other -countries-to-live-with-just-one-parent/

16 https://www.pewresearch.org/fact-tank/2018/04/27/about-one-third-of-u-s-children-are-living-with-an -unmarried-parent/ | Pew Research Center

17 A new Pew Research Center study of 130 countries and territories shows that the U.S. has the world's highest rate of children living in single-parent households.

18 https://www.census.gov/library/stories/2021/04/number-of-children-living-only-with-their-mothers-has -doubled-in-past-50-years.html#:˜:text=With%20Mother%20Only-,Children%20living%20with% 20a%20mother%20only%20is%20the%20second%20most,million%20(21%25)%20in%202020.

of 2020, 21 percent of US children, or about 15.3 million, lived with their mother only—compared to 11 percent, or 7.6 million, in 1968.[19]

And, American Women are Having Fewer Babies

The United States has seen a 50% decline in birth rates —from 25 births per 1,000 people in 1950 to 12 per thousand in 2021.[20] This decline has been underway since about 1960, and birth rates have continued this decline in recent years.

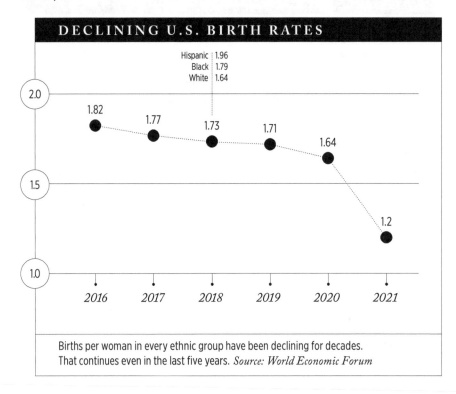

DECLINING U.S. BIRTH RATES

Births per woman in every ethnic group have been declining for decades. That continues even in the last five years. *Source: World Economic Forum*

19 The Boy Crisis: Why Our Boys Are Struggling and What We Can Do About It by Warren Farrell Ph.D. and John Gray | Feb 26, 2019

20 https://www.weforum.org › agenda › 2021 › 07 › declining-fertility-rates-research Why are fertility rates declining in America? | World Economic Forum https://www.weforum.org/agenda/2021/07 /declining-fertility-rates-research/

Section 3: What about Adoption?

In response to our very high rates of unplanned pregnancy, Americans opt for either abortion or single parenting. Many women don't even consider adoption. There are many reasons for this. They believe they can't deal with wondering about where their babies might be for the rest of their lives. Or they're told that they're not strong enough to give birth and then "give up" their baby to others. They couldn't bear the grief and pain. Or there's the shame of a growing, visible stomach when all their family and friends know they're single. Many women believe these myths and aren't encouraged to seriously consider adoption. Many women don't choose adoption because of the guilt they feel, "I could never give away my baby!"

It's an unthinkable option, so they choose between parenting and abortion. Add to that, that American women are having fewer babies. It's no wonder that adoption rates are decreasing. Both domestic infant adoptions and international adoptions are down.

Only One Percent Choose Adoption

Of all the millions of US women who face unplanned pregnancy each year, fewer than about one percent choose to place their babies for adoption.[21] That was the case in 2002, the last year that CDC reported this metric, and appears to be the case still today. Yet currently, there are about two million couples waiting to adopt in the United States, according to both AmericanAdoptions.com and Adoption.com.[22]

---

21 https://adoptioncouncil.org/article/domestic-infant-adoption/
22 https://adoption.com/infants-for-adoption

Domestic Infant Adoptions

Most young women facing unplanned, unwanted pregnancy don't place their babies for adoption. As a result, infant adoption in the US has become very challenging indeed.

- In 2019, there were 25,737 domestic infant adoptions, while there were 916,460 abortions.
- In 2020, there were 16,658 domestic infant adoptions, while there were 930,160 abortions.
- In that year alone,[23] domestic infant adoptions decreased by 35% ,while abortions increased by 1.5%.

WOMEN WHO PLACE FOR ADOPTION	
Pre 1973	9%
Mid 1980's	2%
As of 2002	1%

A decreasing portion of women facing unplanned/unwanted pregnancy place for adoption. *Source: National Center of Health Statistics*

For every child who is placed for adoption, there are as many as 36 families waiting.[24] That average waiting list is getting longer, as abortion and single parenting remain the preferred options and fertility rates decline. The proportion of women who choose to place for adoption remains steady, between 1% and 2% of those facing unplanned, unwanted pregnancies.

International Adoptions

Some prospective parents also pursue international adoption. Typically, the background information and medical history of the child are very limited or unavailable. International adoptions also involve more paperwork to

---

23 Granted, 2020 was an atypical year because of COVID.
24 https://www.americanadoptions.com/pregnant/waiting_adoptive_families

satisfy the regulations of other countries. It takes time to process papers and comply with government requirements, which sometimes include a minimum length of time spent in-country. Given that complexity, it's rare that American couples adopt infants internationally; usually, the children are a bit older. And most international adoptions today are of children with special needs.[25]

Some people do prefer to adopt internationally because they believe there's less risk that birth parents will change their minds. In fact, this happens only *very* rarely in US domestic adoptions. (So rarely, in fact, that there are no data on this—only the occasional, sensationalized story.)

International adoption has also become much more difficult in recent years. Countries that had made up a large portion of our international adoptions, including Russia and China, have cut off American adoptions altogether due to political and diplomatic reasons.

INTERNATIONAL ADOPTIONS IN USA

The number of international adoptions done in the USA peaked in 2004 and has declined since then. *Source: U.S. Department of State & AdoptionNetwork.com*

---

25 https://adoptioncouncil.org/press-release/ncfa-releases-results-of-largest-study-ever-conducted-on-adoptive-parents/

Adoption from Foster Care

Some prospective parents also consider adopting through the foster system. We often hear that the children in the foster system should be placed before we consider reducing abortion rates and/or advocating for adoption. The overall goal of the foster care system, however, is reunification of children with their biological parents.

Adopting through the foster system comes with its own unique set of challenges. Typically, families are separated because the biological parents become temporarily unable to care for the children (because of drugs, prison, abuse, or other circumstances), resulting in the removal of the child from the home. The foster system finds shelter and care for those kids until the family is reunited.

Children in the foster system are not eligible for adoption from foster care until parental rights have been terminated. Therefore, the number of children in foster care who are eligible for adoption is a fraction of the total. The number of children waiting to be adopted also fell in FY 2020 to 117,470.[26] Almost half—57,882 of those—were adopted in 2020. This chart shows the difference between the total number of children in foster care and the number of children available for adoption from foster care.

Reunification —which means getting the family safely back together— is the first goal when a child enters foster care and the most common outcome.[27] After reunification, adoption was the next most common reason for exiting foster care. One-fourth (25%) of all children who exit foster care do so through a permanent adoption.

> ### *Children are not eligible for adoption from foster care until parental rights are terminated, so the number of children available for adoption is a fraction of the total in the foster system.*

"When a child is under three, there is a different process than with older children," explains Katie Mayeda, CEO of Mayeda Consulting in California. "Babies are on a fast track to reunification or adoption due to the need for children to bond with a parent and the adverse effects of attachment disorders.

---

26 https://www.acf.hhs.gov/media/press/2021/national-data-shows-number-children-foster-care
-decreases-third-consecutive-year
27 https://www.childwelfare.gov/pubPDFs/reunification.pdf

In California, biological parents have a shorter timeframe to show that they're committed to finishing their case plans for successful reunification."[28]

The goal of the foster care system is reunification of the child with the birth parents. It serves a worthy purpose, and we are always in need of more foster parents to care for children while they are waiting to rejoin their biological parents. However, if the goal of the hopeful parents is permanent adoption of a child, then these two goals may be at odds with one another. The foster system is not a solution for them.

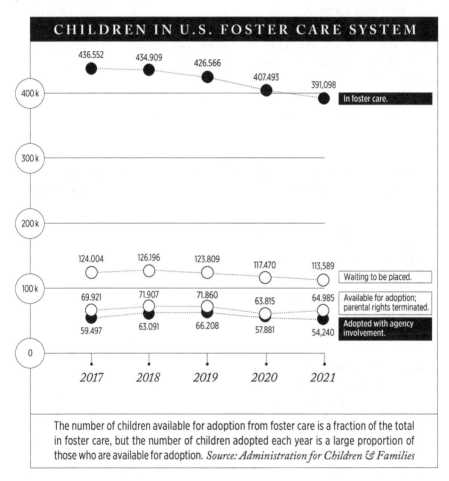

CHILDREN IN U.S. FOSTER CARE SYSTEM

	2017	2018	2019	2020	2021
In foster care.	436.552	434.909	426.566	407.493	391,098
Waiting to be placed.	124.004	126.196	123.809	117.470	113,589
Available for adoption; parental rights terminated.	69.921	71.907	71.860	63.815	64.985
Adopted with agency involvement.	59.497	63.091	66.208	57.881	54,240

The number of children available for adoption from foster care is a fraction of the total in foster care, but the number of children adopted each year is a large proportion of those who are available for adoption. *Source: Administration for Children & Families*

28 *Mayeda Consulting serves nonprofits and government agencies on the front lines of community social work, 'helping the helpers' in public health and criminal justice.* www.mayedaconsulting.com

The Million Dollar Question

The two million American couples waiting to adopt can only hope and pray they'll be able to start families. There are *very* few babies in need of permanent homes and families, *despite the overwhelming number of unwanted pregnancies.* So, the crucial, central question is, *why* do **only one percent** of the women facing unplanned pregnancy choose adoption?

To understand this, I conducted first-hand research over dessert and coffee in my living room. A series of focus groups on this topic included junior high and high school teachers, junior high and high school parents, and youth pastors from various local churches. They acknowledged that several young women in their schools (or groups) get pregnant each year. Often, they were asked for advice; sometimes they were merely observing from the sidelines. In no case, over all those evening conversations, was adoption mentioned by any one of these adults to any of these young women. And if the adults don't suggest it, the young women don't consider it.

> **Most young women don't even consider adoption; it's not suggested to them by the adults who advise them.**

So, why do **only one percent** of the women facing unplanned pregnancy choose adoption?

The short answer, as hard as it was to believe, is this:

a) It simply does not occur to most young women facing unwanted pregnancy to make an adoption plan, and

b) adoption is not suggested to them by the adults to whom they turn for help and advice.

Open adoption is simply not on the radar.

In this book, we'll take a look at the all-new paradigm of US adoption today: how and why it has been completely re-structured in the last three decades. We'll dispel old misconceptions and throw out the baggage associated with them as we learn about current adoption practices.

Then we'll explore the two default options women consider today when facing an unplanned pregnancy. We'll lean into our experiences, research, and findings to update our knowledge about both abortion and single parenting.

With the benefit of hindsight, we'll consider that it's time adoption is seen as a solution for women facing unplanned, unwanted pregnancies—*at least* on par with abortion and single parenting.

Finally, we'll take a look at who would need to embrace this new thinking and how we, as a society, might act on this information.

2

The Adoptions of Yesteryear

"Sealed adoptee birth records are about two things: suppressing truth and promoting fiction. Each one depends on the other."
— #AdopteeRightsLaw

What most people know today about adoption is based on pre-conceptions rooted in the past. Before the 1990s, most adoptions were closed. The woman who gave birth was not allowed an ongoing relationship with her child, and vice versa. In fact, in many cases, the adoption and the very existence of this new person were carefully guarded secrets: all involved shared an unspoken pact never to speak of it again.

Some states set up closed adoptions as a way to protect the birth mother (as well as the birth father and their families) from the child someday finding them and asking questions, or interfering with their lives.

Furthermore, the decision to place for adoption or to parent often was not made by the pregnant woman herself: She may have been forced into adoption, sometimes by her own parents who didn't want the embarrassment: "What would the neighbors say?" The pregnant girl was sent far away to live with a distant relative until the baby was delivered and "given up." Then things could return to "normal."

Sometimes a closed adoption was the preference of the couple adopting because they wanted to pretend that the child was theirs from conception onward. Whether the closed aspect of the adoption was the will of the birth family or the adoptive family, it was a path often chosen out of fear—a fear that being honest would somehow result in rejection, shame, or disapproval. For a myriad of reasons, the adopted child's true story was buried and replaced with a carefully crafted tale.

Secrecy was the hallmark of closed adoptions. And secrets are nearly impossible to keep.

The woman who placed her baby was never able to grieve. Imagine going through the trauma of parting with your child and never being able to talk it out, receive needed help, or heal. She wasn't able to know the next chapter in her baby's life or to stay in touch and see how her baby fared in the new family *she made possible.* Nor did that new family even acknowledge her—or the gift she gave them.

The story just ended, abruptly and without any closure.

The adopted child was often not told that they were adopted. He or she grew up assuming—or being told—that their story was no different than any other child born to any other couple. But the adopted child knows something's off. It's just hard to pinpoint exactly what. Since families aren't good at keeping secrets, the adoptee would usually learn the truth eventually. With that revelation comes a tidal wave of feelings of betrayal: *"My whole life has been a lie!" "My parents did this to me??"*

Then—sometimes still reeling from either that shock or from a sense that he or she was not loved by the birth mother—the adopted child may feel a desire to find and even connect with the birth parents. All children want to know where they came from. All people, in fact, want to know where they came from. It's an innate curiosity that causes children to want to know their story.

For many, some milestone or turning point in their lives sparks the search. It might be their wedding, the birth of their first child, or the marriage of a child. Many search and wonder for years, with no clear path or guidance; many never find any results or closure. Many adoptees only find their birth parents with a great deal of research and effort. That long and painful search is a by-product of closed adoptions.

The search often leads them to sealed adoption records. Each state has different laws about opening these records. Recently, several states have chosen to "unseal" records. Other states don't allow for adoption records to be unsealed and released. Sometimes the records are forever lost—destroyed in fires or moves. In these cases, the curious adoptee is left with many unanswered questions that can be painful for the rest of his/her life.

That is trauma layered on top of trauma. It's no wonder that adoption horror stories abound.

We've come a long way since then.

We now know the harm that was caused by the practice of forced, closed, secret adoptions. Thank God those days are gone! Adoption has successfully evolved into something entirely different today.

A massive shift has taken place. The practice of adoption has completely flipped from the closed adoptions of the 1950s, 60s and 70s to the nearly entirely open adoptions of today. If there is such a thing as a "typical" infant adoption scenario in the US today, that new norm nationwide is called **open adoption**.

3

The Open Adoption Evolution—
A Changed Reality

"He is mine in a way that he will never be hers, yet he is hers in a way that he will never be mine, and so together, we are motherhood."
— Desha Wood

f you do an internet search on "adoption," you're likely to get more hits for pet adoption than for infant adoption.

The average American is only two degrees of separation from someone who was adopted, yet that average person knows little about adoption and how it works today, because it rarely comes up in conversation.

Adoption isn't covered in the news—unless there's some rare occurrence to sensationalize the topic. Adoption isn't discussed over cocktails. It's not among the boxes to check on your dating profile or your driver's license. We just don't talk about adoption, so we don't understand it. Yet, we do have many ingrained preconceptions about adoption.

Let's put some misconceptions to the test. Here's a glimpse into one personal story.

Gwen was a senior in high school when she became pregnant. She had had a feeling she might be pregnant earlier in the year, but pushed the idea to the back of her mind, hoping it would just go away and turn out not to be true. By the time she faced the truth head-on, she estimated she was about 16 weeks along. Three months away from high school graduation, Gwen seriously pondered her options for the first time. Abortion? No, she could not terminate the life growing inside of her. Parenting? Well, that didn't sound good either. She was planning for college and had plans for her own life. Adoption? She didn't know much about how that worked, so she decided to learn a bit about the process.

She found an agency in a nearby town that claimed to facilitate adoptions. She called and gave them a fake name so she could ask a few questions. She was surprised by most of the answers. There were hundreds of couples waiting to adopt, so she would be in the "driver's seat." Would she want to place her baby with a stay-at-home mom or a career mom? A young couple or an older, more established one? A family that already had kids or a childless couple? She could specify race, religion, age, location. It was shocking how many of the decisions would be up to her. Gwen had a lot to think through!

She began reading the profiles of dozens of hopeful adoptive couples before she found the one that met all of her criteria. She was looking for a couple, established in their careers but without children to date—people who could provide a loving home, security on every front. That was her vision.

When Gwen gave birth, she placed her baby into the arms of the couple she chose, creating a family.

The next day, Gwen's heart broke as she watched her baby placed in the car seat. But somehow, deep down, she was confident that she was doing the right thing for her precious new baby girl.

Gwen started classes at the local junior college to stay close to home for a year while she made her plans. The next Fall, she went off to a university and worked intently on her bachelor's degree, graduating three years later on the dean's list. A year after that, Gwen wrote her first letter to the adoptive parents: She was ready to visit.

And so she did. After five years of infrequent contact, the parents welcomed Gwen into their home. She could see that her baby girl was in good hands, happy and healthy. That weekend's visit began a closer connection between the child, her birth mom, and her adoptive parents. Everyone seemed more ready for an ongoing relationship than they were when they parted at the hospital.

Gwen was grateful she was free to pursue her career and stay in touch with the family raising her daughter. After her career was established, she went on to marry and have another child. Knowing her first-born daughter was well taken care of put Gwen at peace.

Does that fit your preconceived ideas about adoption?
Probably not.

The Open Adoption Evolution – A Continuum

4

What does open adoption really mean?

It's actually a *continuum* of openness: Each family navigates the waters until they find the balance of contact and distance that works for them. Visits and privacy are a tradeoff, and geographical distance between the parties will require more work and planning to stay connected. Some want more contact, celebrating holidays in person. Others are satisfied to exchange letters, photos, or social media posts.

At the core of open adoption is a world of *possibilities*. There are an infinite number of ways to structure any ongoing relationship. And adoption is no different. The options are open to embrace and expand upon—or not. And when a family structures these new relationships in the way that works for all, inside the limits of their comfort zone, they know it. They can feel it.

For the Birth Parents

Open adoption means peace of mind. They can rest assured, knowing that their child is thriving with parents who overcame so many hurdles before welcoming their new child into the family. Ideally, the open nature of the adoption allows the birth parents to stay informed about the child's progress.

It often includes ongoing communication between the birth family and the adoptive family. Sometimes, it even allows the birth parents to participate through regular visits.

In some cases, this is worked out gradually and informally. If both the birth parent and the adoptive family want an increased level of contact and visits, they can arrange those get-togethers. In other cases, adoption agencies actually require a set schedule for birth family visits be included in the adoption contract. Sometimes there are negative experiences when the birth family and adoptive family have different expectations and cannot find a compromise. Open adoption works best with open communication.

For the Adoptee

Open adoption means that the child's questions are answered.

The child will first ask, "Why did my Mom choose adoption for me?" The reasons for that choice are as different as each woman who places her child, but the theme running through those stories is that the birth mom was not able to parent at that time in her life, and she loved her child so much that she wanted the best for him or her. She *chose* to place the child's best interests above her own. It's a brave and selfless act of pure love. Learning that the decision was extremely difficult and made from a place of love is very reassuring for a child.

> ## It's a brave and selfless act of pure love.

For the Adoptive Parents

Open adoption means information.

Some adoptive parents are also lucky enough to share the last few months of the pregnancy with the birth parents—they get to know them and gather some insight into their stories. They can also access genetic and medical information to best care for their child. They can provide doctors with fuller history so they can then choose the right course of treatment. It's also possible to gather and preserve cord blood at the birth.[29] It's also helpful to know ancestral histories of various medical and genetic conditions and proclivities, such as alcoholism, asthma, arthritis, diabetes, heart conditions, and certain types of cancer. All of that can be very helpful.

---

29 Scientists believe that these cells may play a role in healing several diseases, including cancer. The cord blood in the umbilical cord and placenta can be collected at birth and placed in storage.

This is not to say that the ideal level of openness for the adoptive family and the birth parents is always the same: It isn't. As with any ongoing relationship, work and communication are required in the hope of finding a balance that works well for all involved.

5

The Open Adoption Evolution – Transparency

"If you tell the truth, you don't have to remember anything."
— Mark Twain

The basic idea underlying open adoption today is transparency. In most cases, children today are aware of their background stories. They know they were adopted and why they were adopted. Their birth mother chose adoption at a time in her life when she felt she could not parent; she was not ready, willing, or able (perhaps all three) to parent well. So, she made the very difficult decision to go forward with her pregnancy, then thoughtfully chose parents for her baby, and then intentionally placed her child with them.

Even when a woman doesn't face pressure to place her child and the adoption is 100% her decision, it's still quite challenging. Most birth mothers describe adoption as the most excruciating, difficult decision they have ever made, but one that they knew, with all their heart, was right.

These women go on to describe the rewards of seeing their baby raised in a happy, stable family. The ability to stay in touch and remain a part of the child's life is one of the key benefits of open adoption. Observing the child's upbringing is also a large part of the healing process for birth parents. After a needed initial grieving period, the visits and other forms of communication can be helpful to both the birth mom and birth father, knowing that their child is well-loved.

> ### *The bottom line is open adoption offers options. It offers connection. It offers answers.*

In addition to providing transparency, another pillar of open adoption is ongoing communication. The transparency of open adoption makes this possible, but whether or not all parties opt to communicate regularly is up to those involved. This usually evolves over time. Some need distance in the first few years after the birth; some bond quickly and become a new extended family sooner.

There are many possible scenarios, and there's no "right" way to do this. Each open adoption is as unique as the humans that comprise it.

The bottom line is open adoption offers options. It offers connection. It offers answers. The people involved can forge the path and set the new traditions that work for them because everything is possible. Staying in touch is possible. Communication is possible. Loving relationships are possible.

And in this world, who would turn down one more person to love them? And one more person to love?

6

New Paradigm, New Language: Words Make a Difference!

"Realize now the power your words command, if you simply choose them wisely."

— Tony Robbins

We've reviewed how much adoption has changed—from the old days when the adoption process was closed to the current, much healthier practice of open adoption. Our language must also change to reflect that shift. For example, when people talk about "giving up a child for adoption," that reference has its roots in the early 1900s. By the end of World War I, orphanages in Boston and New York overflowed. Children were "put up" on the Orphan Train, which then began the trip out West. Each time it stopped in a new town, the children were "put up" on the train's platform so local farmers and craftsmen could survey the kids and choose one (or more) to bring home. More hands at home meant more help in the family business.

Today, it's about people who want to *parent*. They aren't looking for workers. They're looking for family.

Here are some other outdated phrases, and suggestions on how to replace them.

OUTDATED, NEGATIVE TERM	WHY THAT'S AN ISSUE	SUGGESTED REPLACEMENT
"Give up a child for adoption"	Adoption is NOT "giving up."	Place a baby for adoption.
	Delete the word "up"!	Choose adoption.
		Make an adoption plan.
"Keeping the baby"	Objectifies the child.	Choose to parent.
	Diminishes the choice.	
"REAL mother"	An adoptive parent *is* real!	Birth mom or first mom
"REAL dad"	An adoptive parent *is* real!	Birth dad or first dad
"Adoptive parents"	No qualifier needed.	Parents.
"Adopted son"	No qualifier needed.	Son.
"Adopted daughter"	No qualifier needed.	Daughter.
"... is adopted"	Does not define a person.	Was adopted. (as in, a past event)

These are just a few.

Positive adoption language focuses on the person about whom we are speaking, rather than the label we attach to that person, and it shows we value the practice of adoption to build a family. Perhaps the most important reason to phrase things intentionally and choose words carefully is this: Speaking about adoption in a positive, respectful way tells our kids that we value the process by which they've come into our lives.

> ### *Positive adoption language focuses on the person about whom we are speaking, rather than the label.*

You can help spread adoption awareness and encourage others to see adoption in a positive light by using more appropriate vocabulary when talking about adoption.

7

Rejecting the False Dilemma

"If 50 million people believe in a fallacy, it is still a fallacy."
— Prof Samuel Warren Carey

Noun: 'A false dilemma'
    1. a false dichotomy, fallacy
    The false dilemma implies that there are only two options when creative thinking can lead to alternative solutions.
    2. a false premise
    The false premise was set forth to guide the discussion away from the third option.[30]

The current culture in the U.S. presents women with unintended pregnancies with two options: abortion as a safe, quick, painless answer, and (often single) parenting as a glamorous, empowering adventure. Then we dupe women into believing this mirage of "solutions" by withholding the rest of the story.

---

30 https://www.merriam-webster.com/

There is another option!

There are several key reasons that adoption is not seriously considered by women facing unplanned pregnancy today:

- **The idea never even crossed their minds.**
  As discussed, adoption wasn't on the radar, because no one suggested adoption as an option. In most cases, a young woman facing a big decision will consult with either her mom or her partner. If more parents, teachers, pastors, medical professionals—if more people in general—would suggest adoption, this could change. If people are more educated about open adoption, they may be more willing to suggest it in these situations.

- **They don't understand it.**
  Most people don't know much about how adoption works in America today. Some confuse foster care with adoption, and don't know the difference. They don't know how it works, or that they have the power to select a family. They can set their own unique criteria, choosing the parents to ensure that their criteria are met. They may also mistakenly think they will have to cover the medical expenses.

- **They aren't looking at the big picture.**
  Most people don't know there are two million US couples waiting to adopt; there *is* a waiting family.
  Plus, women can't weigh the short-term and long-term effects of all their options when they don't have complete information. They don't know the downsides of abortion and single parenting; they only see the immediate downsides of pregnancy. The adults in their lives are not encouraging them to look at the big picture and consider adoption.

- **They don't know how to get started.**
  The path forward is completely unclear—the costs, the steps, the support—all of it. If women don't know how to envision adoption or how to get started, that, too, is a matter of education. There are many resources in the back of this book, both references and first-hand testimonials, that will explain how to get started and what one would encounter.

- **The potential shame and embarrassment during the pregnancy would be too much.**

  The woman fears the response of her own parents, and/or they fear the shame and embarrassment. Either or both can be factors here. We can only hope that the young woman's parents will, through education and with compassion, learn to put their daughter's long-term health and well-being above their own embarrassment. (An ironic proof point of how hard parenting is!) But this reaction is understandable and common. Many women would rather keep quiet, especially if they think their parents will be angry or ashamed. All the more reason we can benefit from talking openly about this topic before it becomes an issue.

More widespread education and accessible information are needed to enlighten the public so they can better advise, assist and advocate for open adoption.

Read on for a glimpse of how the new norm of open adoption works today. It will be clear why and how adoption in America has changed so much in just the last three decades.

The Adoption Continuum

CLOSED ADOPTION	OPEN ADOPTION
US Adoption used to look like this ...	But adoption can look like this ...

For the Birth Parents

- No info on adoptive parents. - No updates on child's welfare. - Lack of news can be upsetting. - Makes healing from loss harder. - No closure, or ability to affirm decision. - Birth parents worry child feels abandoned, i.e., "Does s/he hate me?" - Questions go unanswered. - No connection can amplify loss and grief.	- Freed from parental responsibilities. - Choose child's parents (same values). - Potential for visits, calls, letters. - Can express their love. - Questions are answered. - Updates help birth parents heal. - Knowing child is loved helps w/ closure. - Stay connected to a family they helped create.

For the Adoptive Parents

- Needed medical history not accessible. - Limited info on allergies, hereditary conditions, etc. - No contact with birth parents. - Must answer child's questions without the needed information.	- Ongoing relationship with birth parents. - Access to medical history as needed. - Understanding birth parents' motivation can help the child understand. - Birth parents available to answer questions - Child knows s/he is loved by all parents.

For the Adoptee

- No contact with birth parents. - Questions why he/she was adopted. - Blame themselves, feel abandoned. - No opportunity to blend families. - Child has more questions than answers.	- Regular in-person visits, calls, letters. - Understands birth parents' decision. - Ongoing connection can help child feel loved, not abandoned. - Understand birth parents' situation. - Relationship with extended family. - Child knows his/her "story."

8

Adoption is HARD

"The greater the obstacle, the more glory in overcoming it."

— Moliere

Years after placement, here's what several birth parents had to say about their decision to choose adoption.

"The year I became a birth mother was the most painful—and the most beautiful year—of my life. I not only gained a son, but also his parents, whom I consider family. You may ask, 'Why would you place your child with adoptive parents after earning a degree?' Well, I wanted him to grow up with an active father. He now has a mom and a dad in the same house to whom he can run in the middle of the night if he has a bad dream. He has a dad who will coach him in sports. He'll grow up knowing what true love is. My son is my greatest accomplishment, and I am so proud to be a part of his life."

"Finding a good family and knowing that it was the answer for me did not make dealing with my choice any easier. Knowing that I would bring this baby into the world and then hand him over to another family was extremely hard but I followed through with my adoption plan because deep down I knew it was for the best for my son."

> ## *I gave her two parents who were financially, physically, and emotionally ready to parent.*

"My daughter chose adoption for her baby. There were times when she questioned if she was doing the right thing, but for the most part, she remained steadfast in her decision, even when challenged by well-meaning friends and family members. I am grateful for her decision, her maturity, her strength, and commitment to stick with the decision that she believed was the very best for her baby and herself. Open adoption is not a legal binding agreement, it is an agreement of respect and trust. My daughter sees her son and his parents two or three times a year. Knowing the loving, nurturing environment in which this little boy is being raised has been a joyful experience. My daughter's decision was the most loving, giving, and honoring thing that any mom could ever do. I am so very proud of her and very grateful for her decision to choose adoption."

"Even though we had an open adoption, I still struggled emotionally after my daughter's birth. I grieved for the child I willingly lost. I had given her something more and better than I could offer at that time in my life. I gave her two parents who were financially, physically, and emotionally ready to parent. I know I made the right decision for my child."

The women and men who choose adoption for their babies do so out of a powerful love. They do work through the difficult times and often emerge stronger on the other side, proud of themselves and embarking on life's next journey. Often the birth parents are happy that their child is being raised by people who are ready, willing, and able to parent well.

Adoption is HARD. Of course it is. The pain is intense. The grief is deep.

Adoption is amazing too. The reward is genuine. The relationships are lasting. And the satisfaction is real.

And thus, this book.

PART TWO

CAN WE TALK?

A CONVERSATION RESET

"May your choices reflect your hopes, not your fears."
— Nelson Mandela

9

Exploring the Inconvenient Truths about our Options

"When you want to help people, you tell them the truth. When you want to help yourself, you tell them what they want to hear."

— Thomas Sowell

Every once in a while, new information causes us to re-examine and re-evaluate societal norms.

During the industrial revolution (1760–1820) and again during World War I (1914–1918), women's roles were stretched beyond the traditional. Now they were bringing home the bacon AND frying it up. When women finally got the right to vote in 1920, positive changes were observed. Child mortality rates decreased by up to 15 percent.[31] Spending on schools increased, as did enrollment.[32] Women, and society at large, benefitted from the change in societal norms.

In another example, use of chewing and smoking tobacco was a widespread habit in this country since its founding. It wasn't until the mid-20th century that the first medical research reports linked smoking to lung cancer. In the 1950s and 1960s, a series of major medical reports confirmed that tobacco caused a range of serious illnesses. Finally, in the 1980s, major advertising campaigns educated the public (remember "No butts"?), and people took to

---

31 https://www.britannica.com/summary/Causes-and-Effects-of-Womens-Suffrage-in-the-United-States
32 Ibid.

heart this new information about the direct link between smoking and cancer. California's smoking population decreased by half in just 20 years, thanks in large part to this campaign. At least as far as smoking goes, people are healthier today and society at large benefitted from this change.

As we learn more, discover more, and uncover more, we want to change social patterns and cultural habits for the better. We WANT to replace yesterday's norms with healthier practices that serve us in the long run.

The same idea can be applied to our response to unplanned pregnancy.

In the last decade or two, more than ever, we have actually *encouraged* abortion and *glamourized* single parenting. We do this by sugar-coating both of those options, downplaying or ignoring their downsides.

As new data emerges, we see compelling reasons to change. The benefits of change are illuminated, if we don't turn away. Even with the new data at hand, it can be hard to see the long-term consequences of our past ways, unless you are intentional about it.

With the benefit of hindsight, we see trends forming in the rear view mirror as we arrive at a place we may not want to be. Acknowledging the false dilemma is inconvenient. So is exploring what it has cost us.

Could the long-term consequences of that binary choice impact you? Or a woman you love? Let's be brave and review them.

10

Let's be Honest:
The Challenges of Single Parenting

"Biology is the least of what makes someone a mother."

— Oprah Winfrey

The woman facing unplanned pregnancy and considering whether to abort or to parent is most likely single.

According to a May 2016, Guttmacher.org[33] report, only about 14% of abortion patients are married, and an additional 31% were cohabiting. A slight majority were not living with a partner in the month they became pregnant; forty-six percent had never married and 9% had previously been married.[34] (Although there is a slow but steady trend (1975-2019) among married women to choose abortion, they are still a minority.) For these reasons, and to simplify, the parenting option will be discussed here as "single parenting."

Solo Parenting

As we covered in chapter one, more people are deciding to take on single parent roles. The increase in the number of women having children outside of marriage has been significant over the last 50-60 years. In 1960 only 5% of mothers were unmarried and in 2015, that rate was 41%. (Refer back to

---

33 The Alan Guttmacher Institute is Planned Parenthood's research affiliate.
34 https://www.guttmacher.org › report › characteristics-us-abortion-patients-2014

Chart 3).[35] That's an increase of over 800%. As a result, many more children are living with solo parents. On average, 6.8% of children around the world under the age of 18 live in a single-parent household. But in the US, that number is 23%. A recent 2019 Pew Research Center study of 130 countries and territories shows that the U.S. has taken the first-place position for the world's highest rate of children living in single-parent households.[36]

And the rise in births to unmarried women is celebrated.

The stigma surrounding single motherhood used to discourage women from choosing that option.[37] The message from Hollywood is that single moms are the personification of female liberation and independence. Article after article inspires awe for the woman who triumphs as a single mom, from Parenting Magazine[38] to Ranker.com.[39]

Bucking the trend, popular magazine Evie published "The Celebrity Lie Of Single-Mom Life As Glamorous And Empowering" in May 2021. In that article, Lisa Britton described ". . . numerous starlets [are] flaunting their solo-motherhood lifestyles on Instagram, making things seem glamorous and easy,"[40] while avoiding posting anything negative about their situations. Hollywood is framing solo motherhood as a form of female empowerment. "Week 2 of solo parenting and you can pretty much call me superwoman now LOL. . . ." One sperm bank who shall remain nameless touts, "We are very proud and happy to help single mothers having their dream of a child come true."[41]

> *Hollywood is framing solo motherhood as a form of female empowerment.*

However, these situations apply mainly to wealthy and somewhat older women. That same article pointed out that single mother households are far more likely to live in poverty and become food insecure.[42]

35 National Vital Statistics Report from CDC
36 Religion and household makeup around the world | Pew Research Center https://www.pewresearch.org/religion/2019/12/12/religion-and-living-arrangements-around-the-world/
37 *The ATLANTIC. Why So Many Women Choose Abortion Over Adoption.* By Olga Khazan MAY 20, 2019
38 https://www.parenting.com/pregnancy/celebrity-single-moms/
39 https://www.ranker.com/list/most-famous-single-moms-in-hollywood/celebrity-lists
40 The Celebrity Lie Of Single-Mom Life As Glamorous And Empowering | Evie Magazine https://www.eviemagazine.com/post/the-celebrity-lie-of-single-mom-life-as-glamorous-and-empowering
41 IBID
42 IBID.

Later in life, some women who choose to be single moms when their careers are on solid ground. That's very different from the teen who chooses to parent without a partner, without an education, AND without a career. As a result,

More Children are Living with a Solo MotherOnce largely limited to poor women and minorities, single motherhood is now becoming a new "norm." This prevalence is due in part to the growing trend of children born outside marriage—a societal trend that was virtually unheard of decades ago. Single motherhood has grown so common in America that today more than 80 percent of single-parent families are headed by single mothers—and nearly a third live in poverty.

In an effort to highlight a growing problem in America, then-Senator Barack Obama drove this point home in his June 2008 Father's Day talk in Chicago. In his speech that day he said:

"Of all the rocks upon which we build our lives, we are reminded today that family is the most important. And we are called to recognize and honor how critical every father is to that foundation. They are teachers and coaches. They are mentors and role models. They are examples of success and the men who constantly push us toward it.

But if we are honest with ourselves, we'll admit that what too many fathers also are, is missing—missing from too many lives and too many homes. They have abandoned their responsibilities, acting like boys instead of men. And the foundations of our families are weaker because of it.

You and I know how true this is in the African American community. We know that more than half of all black children live in single-parent households, a number that has doubled—doubled—since we were children. We know the statistics—that children who grow up without a father are:

- Five times more likely to live in poverty and commit crime;
- Nine times more likely to drop out of schools;
- Twenty times more likely to end up in prison.

They are more likely to have behavioral problems or run away from home or become teenage parents themselves. And the foundations of our community are weaker because of it." [43]

---

43 Then-Senator Barack Obama June 15, 2008, Father's Day speech, Chicago
 https://www.politico.com/story/2008/06/text-of-obamas-fatherhood-speech-011094

41

The American family is changing in many ways: Cohabitation is on the rise,[44] more adults are delaying or foregoing marriage, and a growing share of children are living with an unmarried parent.[45] In the U.S., about one-in-five children overall (21%) are living with a solo mother, up from 12% in 1968.[46]

Single-Mother Households Are Far More Likely to Live in Poverty

The tough reality is that single-mother households are far more likely to be poor than married-couple households. The poverty rate for single-mother families in 2018 was 34%, more than five times higher than the rate for married-couple families, which was only 6%.[47] Nearly three-in-five (58 percent) of all poor children lived in families headed by unmarried mothers. And one-in-three single moms spend over 50% of their income on housing, while 27% struggle to afford shelter. Forty percent of single moms in the U.S. have jobs that provide low wages and no paid leave. Almost one-third of single-mother families are food insecure.[48] Two out of three single moms receive reduced price or free meals. Among the homeless families in America, more than 80%[49] were headed by single women with children.

It's a grim picture of a hard life. Yet, it's reality for those who don't have the resources of someone like Angelina Jolie, Mindy Kaling, or Sandra Bullock.

The Effect on the Children

Parents who get and stay married tend to be different in many other important respects from single parents—including having more time, education, and income—and it may be these differences that lie behind the gaps in their children's success, rather than the fact of marriage itself.

---

44 The landscape of marriage and cohabitation in the U.S. https://www.pewresearch.org /social-trends/2019/11/06/the-landscape-of-marriage-and-cohabitation-in-the-u-s/

45 About one-third of U.S. children are living with an unmarried parent | Pew Research Center https://www.pewresearch.org/fact-tank/2018/04/27/about-one-third-of-u-s-children-are-living -with-an-unmarried-parent/

46 Ibid.

47 PovertySnapshot2019-2.pdf (nwlc.org) https://nwlc.org/resources/national-snapshot-poverty -among-women-families-2019/

48 Single Mother Statistics (UPDATED 2022) (singlemotherguide.com) https://singlemotherguide .com/single-mother-statistics/

49 more than 80% https://bridgeofhopeinc.org/family-homelessness-in-the-united-states/

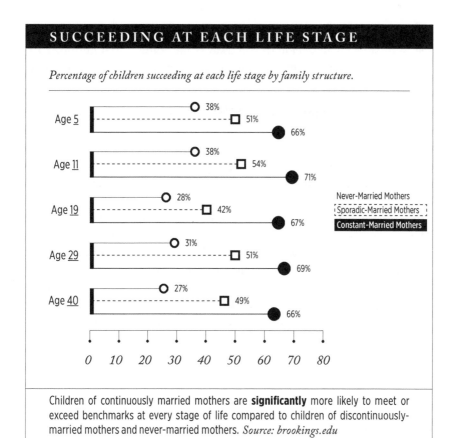

SUCCEEDING AT EACH LIFE STAGE

Percentage of children succeeding at each life stage by family structure.

Age 5 — ○ 38% ▫ 51% ● 66%

Age 11 — ○ 38% ▫ 54% ● 71%

Age 19 — ○ 28% ▫ 42% ● 67%

Age 29 — ○ 31% ▫ 51% ● 69%

Age 40 — ○ 27% ▫ 49% ● 66%

0 10 20 30 40 50 60 70 80

Never-Married Mothers
Sporadic-Married Mothers
Constant-Married Mothers

Children of continuously married mothers are **significantly** more likely to meet or exceed benchmarks at every stage of life compared to children of discontinuously-married mothers and never-married mothers. *Source: brookings.edu*

It's not only the adults who pay the price of single parenting. The Brookings Institute research shows that family structure plays a big role in the success of children at various stages of life, as evidenced by their data. Children at every age have a greater chance of success in a home where the mother is married, and a lesser chance of success in homes of never-married mothers. Children raised by married parents typically do better in life on almost every measure.[50]

In the United States, 24.7 million children live in a home where their biological father is not present. That equates to one in every three children in America.[51] According to the U.S. Department of Justice, 85% of children

---

50 Read more about both of those effects on kids here: The marriage effect: Money or parenting? (brookings.edu)

51 https://www.npr.org/sections/ed/2017/06/18/533062607/poverty-dropouts-pregnancy-suicide -what-the-numbers-say-about-fatherless-kids

who exhibit some type of behavioral disorder come from a fatherless home, as do 90% of youth who decide to run away from home.[52] In addition, 75% of the long-term correctional facility inmates are from father-absent households.[53]

Boys from Fatherless Homes

According to the Federal Bureau of Prisons, 93% of our prison inmates are male[54] and more than half[55] of the youth in prison grew up without their father. Children who live in a single-parent homes are more than twice as likely to die from suicide.[56]

In his article, "Why Young Men Become Shooters," Park MacDougald writes, "Whatever the nominal motivations behind them, rampage shootings are nearly always a product of wounded masculinity."[57] He quotes Ralph Larkin, a criminologist at John Jay College who has studied mass shootings for decades: "They are the most masculine of crimes."[58] Warren Farrell, author and chair of the Coalition to Create a White House Council on Boys and Men, states, "There's common denominators among mass shooters. The most obvious is that they're male—98 percent are male."[59]

A second common denominator is that they're almost all dad-deprived males, Farrell continues. "What we think of when we think of mass shootings is the people who are hurt. We don't realize that all of these people are hurt by boys who are hurt, who are deprived of their dads, who are feeling neglected and depressed."[60]

Fathers are an important component in helping young males grow into productive men.

52 The Problem — Young Warriors www.youngwarriors.org/the-problem
53 IBID
54 https://www.bop.gov/about/statistics/statistics_inmate_gender.jsp
55 Survey of Youth in Residential Placement: Youth Characteristics and Backgrounds (ojp.gov)
    https://www.ojp.gov/pdffiles1/ojjdp/grants/250753.pdf
56 https://www.webmd.com/baby/news/20030123/absent-parent-doubles-child-suicide-risk
57 https://unherd.com/2022/05/why-young-men-become-shooters/
58 Ibid. and Larkin, Ralph. Masculinity, School Shooters, and the Control of Violence
    https://www.researchgate.net/publication/226359341_Masculinity_School_Shooters_and_the
    _Control_of_Violence
59 Ibid.
60 Ibid.

Girls from Fatherless Homes

Girls need their dads too. Daughters from fatherless homes are four times more likely to get pregnant as teenagers[61] And *twice as likely* to suffer from obesity.[62] They're far more likely to struggle with bad relationships, eating disorders, and depression. These glaring statistics paint a dreary, difficult picture of single motherhood for their children.

As with all our options, there are also downsides to single parenting for the mother. Furthermore, if a woman drops out of school to have and raise a child, the picture is even more bleak. Single parenting is challenging—and even more so if one's education ends midway, undermining career and job growth opportunities before they've begun.

Summary: Let's Be Honest about Single Parenting

One thing is certain: The women who choose to raise a baby on their own, thinking it will be fun and glamourous, are starting on a long, arduous road. There may or may not be extended family support. Almost all will find that life as a single mom is an unimaginable amount of hard work. It's exhausting and expensive.

Most women will find a way to make it work, mustering more strength and resolve than they ever knew they possessed. Many will rise to the challenge of raising children on their own and become some of the best mothers ever. It is doable, of course. It's just not fun or glamourous for the single parent.

In addition, the child faces an uphill struggle that is not of his or her own making. He or she starts out with disadvantages to overcome, just by the nature of the family structure.

The eventual outcomes and consequences of the massive shift toward single parenting—that we could not have predicted in the 1970s—come with significant disadvantages. The last few decades' revelations about single parenting and how those children are doing over the long-term are worth consideration. They weigh into the big picture when we're considering our options with complete information.

---

61 https://journals.sagepub.com/doi/abs/10.1177/0192513X03255346?journalCode=jfia&
62 Ibid.

11

Let's be Honest:
The Impact of Abortion on Women

"When you want to help people, you tell them the truth.
When you want to help yourself, you tell them what they want
to hear."

— Thomas Sowell

*"In reality 73.8% of women who have ended a pregnancy say they were not suf-
ficiently informed about their options beforehand."*[63]

L et's be honest about the impact of abortion on women. Really.
We see unplanned pregnancy as a problem to be solved. And
we're told that abortion is a quick solution to that problem. And
that's true—just a half day appointment will do it, no time off work required.
We can tell from the numerous people who are very public about their procedure that it is quite socially acceptable. And no one is the wiser. The short-
term benefit of choosing abortion, especially the convenience, is compelling.

Society tells us that there's no downside to abortion. *That* is simply not true.

While we recognize that there are some risks to full term pregnancy and
delivery, many people do not know or acknowledge that abortion also carries
risks to a woman's health. Elective abortions can exact an immense physical
and emotional toll on women later in life, and also on their future pregnancies.

---

63 Journal of American Physicians and Surgeons, 11-4-2017

Most women who undergo abortion procedures are not aware of the long-term effects, but numerous studies have documented them in three categories—compromised mental health, preterm births, and increased risk of breast cancer.

Compromised Mental Health

Hundreds of US studies have extensively examined the association between abortion and mental health. The most comprehensive sources appear to be the research done by Dr. David C Reardon, Dr. Priscilla Coleman, and the American Association of Pro-Life Obstetricians and Gynecologists, known as AAPLOG.[64]

Both pro-life and pro-choice researchers agree that "the abortion experience directly contributes to mental health problems."[65] The larger studies done with nationally representative samples and a variety of controls for personal and situational factors indicate abortion significantly increases risk for the following mental health problems: [66]

- Depression
- Anxiety
- Substance abuse
- Suicide ideation and behavior[67]

Suicide, specifically, is a serious risk, based on the much-studied correlation. Young women, under 18 years old, account for 15–30% of abortions and have a significantly higher suicide rate than their peers: compared with women who delivered, women were 6.5 times more likely to die by suicide during the

---

64 AAPLOG, *the* American Association of Pro-Life Obstetricians and Gynecologists. (www.aaplog.org/)
     AAPLOG 's mission is to encourage and equip its members and other concerned medical
     practitioners to defend the lives of both the pregnant mother and her pre-born child.
65 National Library of Medicine, National Center for Biotechnology Information.
     https://www.ncbi.nlm.nih.gov/pmc/articles/PMC6207970/
     Article: The abortion and mental health controversy: A comprehensive literature review of common
     ground agreements, disagreements, actionable recommendations, and research opportunities by David
     C Reardon
66 AAPLOG Practice Bulletin No. 7, Abortion and Mental Health, December 30, 2019. FINAL-Abortion
     -Mental-Health-PB7.pdf (aaplog.org)
     https://aaplog.org/wp-content/uploads/2019/12/FINAL-Abortion-Mental-Health-PB7.pdf
67 IBID.

year after an induced abortion.[68] AAPLOG says that another large study found a 155% increase in suicidal behavior post-abortion.[69]

"Literally every large scale study of the abortion and mental health link has revealed higher rates of mental illness among women."[70] In fact, the largest study to date incorporating data from 22 individual studies indicates quite consistently that abortion is associated with moderate to highly increased risks of psychological problems subsequent to the procedure.[71]

For many women who've chosen abortion, reconciling with the decision is a life-long endeavor. As Dr. Coleman also notes in a 2015 interview, she found that about 50% of women who have abortions do believe that they are "terminating the life of a human being," and that belief tends to make the aftermath more traumatic. As ultrasound technology continues to improve, we're able to clearly see the human formation even earlier.

About 80% of Americans view biologists as the group most qualified to determine when a human's life begins. A recent survey of 5577 biologists from 1,058 academic institutions around the world showed a consensus: 96% of those experts in biology agree that human life begins at fertilization.[72] That makes it increasingly difficult for a pregnant women to deny that she is carrying a human life, a dissonance which can lead to compromised mental health issues and even PTSD-like trauma.

Dr. David C Reardon comments on the inherent biases of even the scientists involved in the research, how it affects their interpretation of the data, and whether they emphasize or minimize the risks associated with abortion.

> "Still, both sides agree that (a) abortion is consistently associated with elevated rates of mental illness compared to women without a history of abortion; (b) the abortion experience directly contributes to mental health problems for at least some women; (c) there are risk factors, such as pre-existing mental illness, that identify women at greatest risk of mental health problems after an abortion; and (d) it is impossible to conduct research in this field in a manner that can

---

68 Reardon, David C., et al. "Deaths associated with pregnancy outcome: a record linkage study of low income women." Southern Medical Journal, vol. 95, no. 8, Aug. 2002, pp. 834+. Gale Academic OneFile. Accessed 26 Oct. 2022.

69 https://aaplog.org/resources/patient-brochures/

70 Reardon DC, Craver C. Effects of Pregnancy Loss on Subsequent Postpartum Mental Health: A Prospective Longitudinal Cohort Study. International Journal of Environmental Research and Public Health. 2021; 18(4):2179. https://doi.org/10.3390/ijerph18042179

71 https://doi.org/10.1192/bjp.bp.110.077230 Published online by Cambridge University Press page 183

72 Jacobs, Steven and Jacobs, Steven, The Scientific Consensus on When a Human's Life Begins (November 29, 2021). Jacobs, S.A., The Scientific Consensus on When a Human's Life Begins, Issues in Law & Medicine, Volume 36, Number 2, 2021., Available at SSRN: https://ssrn.com/abstract=3973608

definitively identify the extent to which any mental illnesses following abortion can be reliably attributed to abortion in and of itself. "[73]

Of course, mental health risks can be difficult to decipher, because often poor social support and difficult life circumstances can factor into a woman's decision to have an abortion, and these can affect her mental health as well.[74]

Dr. Reardon concludes, ". . .Risk factors identifying women who are at greater risk, (including a history of prior mental illness,) can be used to identify women who may benefit from more pre-abortion and post-abortion counseling.[75]

There are post-abortive care and support groups offline and on social media, particularly on Facebook, that give women a place to talk with others and share their experience.

The Rachel's Vineyard retreat I observed was attended by 19 women, ranging in age from their 20s to their 80s and every single age group in between. It made a lasting impression on me that women in their 70s and 80s were sobbing as they shared their stories. They were still grieving their abortions, many decades later. With the help of these programs, many are finally able to get closure, heal and move on with their lives.[76]

AAPLOG makes this recommendation: All women who present for elective abortion should be screened for risk factors for adverse mental health outcome and these risk factors discussed with the patient as part of informed consent.[77]

---

73 National Library of Medicine, National Center for Biotechnology Information. https://www.ncbi.nlm .nih.gov/pmc/articles/PMC6207970/ Article: The abortion and mental health controversy: A comprehensive literature review of common ground agreements, disagreements, actionable recommendations, and research opportunities by David C Reardon.

74 AAPLOG Practice Bulletin No. 7, Abortion and Mental Health, December 30, 2019. FINAL -Abortion-Mental-Health-PB7.pdf (aaplog.org) https://aaplog.org/wp-content/uploads/2019/12/FINAL-Abortion-Mental-Health-PB7.pdf

75 Dr. David C Reardon, Oct. 29, 2018, National Library of Medicine, National Center for Biotechnology Information. https://www.ncbi.nlm.nih.gov/pmc/articles/PMC6207970/ Article: The abortion and mental health controversy: A comprehensive literature review of common ground agreements, disagreements, actionable recommendations, and research opportunities by David C Reardon.

76 (https://www.rachelsvineyard.org/)

77 FINAL-Abortion-Mental-Health-PB7.pdf (aaplog.org) https://aaplog.org/wp-content/uploads/2019/12/FINAL-Abortion-Mental-Health-PB7.pdf

Preterm Births

Abortion increases the risk of very preterm births—that is babies born between 22 and 26 weeks, at the edge of life—for any future, wanted pregnancy.

As of November 2021, 168 studies have been published on the association between abortion and preterm birth (PTB).[78] These tiny babies require neonatal intensive care support to survive, and many of the 22–24 week-old babies don't survive. Very premature births of post-abortive women result in over three million infant deaths worldwide each year.

AAPLOG writes on their findings[79]:
- First trimester induced abortion is one of the top three risk factors for preterm births.
- Surgical abortions are associated with a "dose effect," meaning an increased number of abortions confer increasing risk of PTB (because the cervix is weakened with each subsequent procedure).
- Two or more abortions increase a woman's risk of future preterm birth by up to 93%, and her risk of VERY preterm birth by more than 200%.
- Preterm births can have health risks for a baby. Vital organs have not had enough time to fully develop. Also, preterm birth leads to an increased risk for short and long term complications such as cerebral palsy, impaired vision and/or hearing and impaired cognitive development.

The Royal College of Obstetrics and Gynecology (RCOG) acknowledges the association of surgical abortion and PTB, as does the AAPLOG. Despite the evidence presented in these 168 peer-reviewed science-based studies, the largest providers of abortions in the US do not inform patients of the association between surgical abortion and later preterm births. AAPLOG recommends that information about the increased risk of preterm births after surgical abortion should be included in informed consent practices prior to surgical abortion.

---

78 PB-5-Overview-of-Abortion-and-PTB.pdf (aaplog.org)
   https://aaplog.org/wp-content/uploads/2021/11/PB-5-Overview-of-Abortion-and-PTB.pdf
79 Ibid.

Increased Risk of Breast Cancer

In their Committee *Opinion 8: Abortion and Breast Cancer*, AAPLOG states:

> *"The protective effect of a full-term pregnancy on breast cancer risk has been known since the Middle Ages when it was noted that nuns had a higher risk of breast cancer than women with children. Medical authorities agree that a full-term pregnancy lowers a woman's risk of breast cancer. . . . These facts are not controversial and are acknowledged by all medical organizations."*[80]

Furthermore, an abortion-breast cancer link passes every one of the standard Bradford-Hill Criteria[81] which determine if causation can be deduced.

> *"Most scientists will acknowledge a cause-and-effect relationship if the events meet the Bradford-Hill Criteria for causation. This test was used in 1964 by the U.S. Surgeon General to determine causality of cigarettes in lung cancer promotion. These same criteria have been fulfilled by the world's epidemiologic studies of the abortion breast cancer link."*[82]

America was not content to blindly follow when the tobacco industry denied a link between tobacco and lung cancer, based on its own studies. AAPLOG suggests applying the same wisdom here.

Additionally, there is a scientific, biologically plausible mechanism for breast cancer promotion caused by electively terminating a normal pregnancy. Here's that explanation in a nutshell:

> Over the course of a woman's life, her breast tissue will develop into four different types of lobules.
>
> All women are born with Type 1 lobules, which mature into Type 2 lobules at puberty. The lobules type is important to note because 99% of all breast cancers arise in Types 1 & 2 lobules. Types 3 & 4 lobules are resistant to breast cancer.
>
> During the first 24 weeks of pregnancy, she will see a sharp increase in the development of Type 2 lobules. Beginning at 20 weeks, her Type 2 lobules will begin to mature into Type 4 lobules. As pregnancy continues beyond 32 weeks,

---

80 https://aaplog.org/wp-content/uploads/2020/01/FINAL-CO-8-Abortion-Breast-Cancer-1.9.20.pdf
81 The Bradford-Hill Criteria for causation are strength, consistency, specificity, temporality, biological gradient, plausibility, coherence. experiment and analogy.
82 https://aaplog.org/wp-content/uploads/2020/01/FINAL-CO-8-Abortion-Breast-Cancer-1.9.20.pdf

70-90% of her breast tissue has matured into Type 4 lobules by week 40, and the risk of future breast cancer is reduced. There is a 90% risk reduction when she carries a pregnancy to term compared to if she remained childless.[83]

After lactation ceases, the breast forms Type 3 lobules. After menopause, these Type 3 lobules regress to Type 1 lobules, but the protection gained from earlier term pregnancies is permanent and provides lifelong protection to these Type 1 lobules.

What's the Risk?

Ending a pregnancy before 32 weeks stops the Type 2 lobules from developing into Type 4 lobules. *That is, ending a pregnancy early stops breast development at a time when there is an increased amount of cancer-vulnerable Type 2 lobules.*

The longer a woman maintains Types 1 and/or 2 lobules, the higher her risk of breast cancer.

The Bradford-Hill Criteria for causation, together with the above explanation (that ending a pregnancy before 32 weeks stops the Type 2 lobules from developing into Type 4 lobules), offers strong evidence of the link between abortion and breast cancer. Ethical medical practice obligates a physician to counsel a woman considering abortion that this decision may increase the risk of breast cancer later in life.[84]

---

83 *Note: But if she never got pregnant, she would not have experienced that initial increase in the development of Type 2 lobules during the first 24 weeks of pregnancy.*

84 For more information, please see the January 2020 publication, "Abortion and Breast Cancer" https://aaplog.org/wp-content/uploads/2020/01/FINAL-CO-8-Abortion-Breast-Cancer-1.9.20.pdf

Chemical abortions

In 2000 the FDA approved the two-drug "abortion pill," and women have been able to perform their own early abortions—up to 10 weeks of gestation—without leaving their homes.

First, the woman takes the mifepristone pill, or RU-486. Then, 24 to 48 hours later, the woman takes misoprostol or Cytotec. Together, these drugs induce delivery.[85]

(Note that some women do change their minds about the ending their pregnancy. In this case, an "abortion pill reversal" is possible within the first 24 hours after taking that first pill.[86])

As of 2020, medication abortion accounted for the majority (54%) of US abortions,[87] so recent changes in policy here are worth noting. In 2021, the FDA made it easier to get a chemical abortions by phone:

- The "in-person dispensing requirement" ~ stating that mifepristone be given only in health-care settings such as clinics, medical offices, and hospitals ~ was removed.
- A requirement was added, stating that pharmacies dispensing the drug be certified.

Verifying that a pharmacy is certified does not replace in-person medical care. If the procedure is done at home, without a medical exam and without an ultrasound, then:

- The viability of her pregnancy cannot be confirmed. If the pregnancy is ectopic (in the fallopian tube), she'll need specialized medical care.
- The stage of her pregnancy is not confirmed. In practice, women are often unsure how far along they are. If she's past that ten-week maximum, attempting a chemical abortion at home can be dangerous.
- Taking these pills alone at home, she may be far from emergency medical care when it's needed, which is often.

Intense pain, bleeding, and contractions may last for days and necessitate intervention: "Seventeen states maintain records of state Medicaid reimbursements for abortions and subsequent emergency room ("ER") treatment within 30 days of the abortion. Based on this data, in 2015, the rate of ER visits per 1,000 women who underwent a chemical abortion in the past 30 days was

---

85 https://www.youtube.com/watch?v=j0tQZhEisaE&ab_channel=fsbcjc Noted board-certified OB/GYN Dr. Anthony Levatino testified before the US House of Representatives Committee on the Judiciary in 2015 and lead Congress through the steps.

86 AbortionPillReversal.com

87 https://www.guttmacher.org/article/2022/02/medication-abortion-now-accounts -more-half-all-us-abortions

an astonishing 354.8."[88] Thirty-five percent go to the ER after attempting an abortion at home. Women taking these drugs at home alone, without medical supervision or access to a doctor, may be risking their health. And at-home, chemical abortions are growing quickly as requests for mail-order abortion pills surged after the Roe reversal.

Summary: Let's Be Honest about Abortion

The short-term and long-term effects on women from induced abortion—compromised mental health, increased risk of preterm births, and increased risk of breast cancer—are not well known. The dangers of at-home chemical abortions are also not well known. But they should be. Medical professionals are obligated to provide relevant information about the effects of abortion on women prior to any procedure as a matter of "informed consent." In the area of abortion, they simply don't.

Experts can interpret the same data in ways that either minimize or emphasize the negative effects of abortion on a woman's health. There is a broad spectrum of expert views and biases, and sometimes it's hard to know which "experts" to believe, and which biases to ignore. When considering the effects of abortion on the mental, emotional and physical health of women, it's important to consider the source of your information.

In our earlier tobacco example, the first medical research reports in the 1950s linked smoking to lung cancer. In the 1960s, a series of major medical reports confirmed that tobacco caused a range of serious illnesses. Finally, in the 1980s, the US smoking population began to decrease significantly after widespread public service campaigns. But it was slow progress over the course of decades because the tobacco companies that benefited financially were the very ones telling Americans that smoking was harmless and chic.

The AAPLOG points out that many of the foundations funding the studies that minimize these links are also the very same organizations that donate to promote abortion and fund the abortion industry itself.[89]

We don't do women any favors by suggesting that abortion is a quick, easy solution without negative, lasting effects on the women we love.

---

88 https://journals.sagepub.com/doi/pdf/10.1177/23333928211053965 A Longitudinal Cohort Study of Emergency Room Utilization Following Mifepristone Chemical and Surgical Abortions, 1999-2015
89 For more detailed information, refer to Abortion and Mental Health: https://aaplog.org/wp-content/uploads/2019/12/FINAL-Abortion-Mental-Health-PB7.pdf Abortion and Preterm Birth: https://aaplog.org/wp-content/uploads/2021/11/PB-5-Overview-of-Abortion-and-PTB.pdf Abortion and Breast Cancer: https://aaplog.org/wp-content/uploads/2020/01/FINAL-CO-8-Abortion-Breast-Cancer-1.9.20.pdf

A Fresh Look at Adoption

In almost three million unplanned pregnancies each year, the vast majority are choosing between abortion and parenting. Only a tiny fraction choose adoption. They become "birth parents".

Many of today's birth parents also become enthusiastic advocates of open adoption. They reject the binary choice. They say, Let's be honest about the social and behavioral ramifications and outcomes of single parenting. And let's be honest about the effects of abortion on women's mental and physical health, and the health of her future pregnancies.

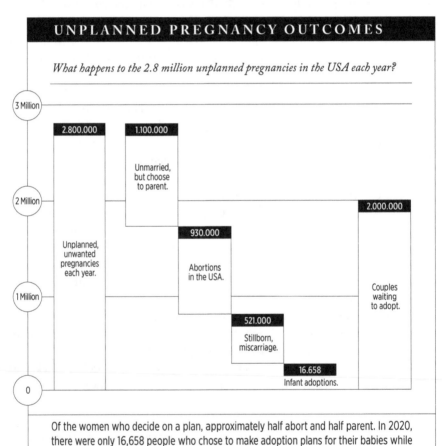

UNPLANNED PREGNANCY OUTCOMES

What happens to the 2.8 million unplanned pregnancies in the USA each year?

3 Million

2.800.000 — Unplanned, unwanted pregnancies each year.

1.100.000 — Unmarried, but choose to parent.

2 Million

2.000.000 — Couples waiting to adopt.

930.000 — Abortions in the USA.

1 Million

521.000 — Stillborn, miscarriage.

16.658 — Infant adoptions.

0

Of the women who decide on a plan, approximately half abort and half parent. In 2020, there were only 16,658 people who chose to make adoption plans for their babies while approximately 2 million couples are waiting to adopt. *Source: US Census Bureau*

Let's take better care of the women we love. Help them avoid the life-long side effects of today's two choices. And help ensure they won't be attending retreats to deal with decades-long regret in their golden years.

We've learned so much about the unintended outcomes of both abortion and single parenting. And we've learned so much about how to do adoption well. And we know that there are millions of couples ready and hoping to adopt. These must weigh into the big picture when considering the options with complete information.

We can do better. We should change this dynamic.

Curious about how it works? Read the true stories of those living in open adoptions.

PART THREE
THE ADOPTION TRIAD

A Closer Look at Adoption Today – Exploring the Triad

At the core of any adoption is a trio of people:
the adoptive parent(s),
the adoptee themselves, and
the birth parents - the woman who gave birth and her male partner.

So, how does open adoption work in the US today? What does it mean when a woman *chooses* to make an adoption plan?

In order to explore the main facets of adoption today and get insight into the dynamics, we need to look at it from three different perspectives—that of the woman who gives birth, the adoptive parents, and the adoptee.

We'll start with the birth parent perspective. It's the woman facing unplanned pregnancy and her partner who make the decision to create an adoption plan. Those are the people who will ultimately need our support, both before and after placement. That's where the energy, education, empathy, and resources are desperately required. Then, we'll take a look at the perspectives of adoptees, and their reflections on life inside their adoptive family. We will end with the adoptive parent perspective—the ones who receive the gift of family when adoption is chosen. That's my firsthand experience.

We will examine each of these three different perspectives through a collection of true, first-person anecdotes. These stories will uncover the inner thoughts, concerns, and discoveries lived out by each person in the adoption triad. Prepare yourself to go deep into their psyches for a unique and maybe even surprising view into the hearts and souls of these human beings.

To be sure, the journey will provide an eye-opening glimpse into how open adoption can work today.

12

The Birth Parent Perspective

"A woman is like a tea bag—you don't know how strong she is until she's in hot water."

— Eleanor Roosevelt

Any woman considering placing her baby for adoption will naturally have a thousand questions about how the process works and what the future will look like. Most parents would agree that there is no perfect parent. The entire parenting job is scary and messy and endless. Even in the best of conditions, parenting is an all-consuming, emotional, unpredictable endeavor. Any young woman trying to evaluate her options and see into the future naturally has many questions about what to expect.

Reading the stories of other birth moms will help shed light on those questions. Others' experiences can help one to get perspective and also to gain hope. When women write their birth mom story a few years later, the passing of time often results in a different outlook. That matured hindsight perspective may be helpful to women facing this decision, as they try to sort out their options and muster the courage to place their babies. These stories can also reassure women and give them reason to be optimistic.

Understanding the process and reading others' stories, however, does not alleviate the pain and grief that come from losing a child, even to adoption. For many birth moms, the sorrow can last a lifetime. We must acknowledge that. Many birth moms are comforted by knowing that their child is doing well. Some are comforted by ongoing contact. Some are even blessed with a newly extended family.

Some professionals in the adoption community are (finally!) beginning to talk more about the need for birth mother support. Even the monumental shift from closed to open adoptions did not bring with it much improved support for these brave women who choose adoption. That is a "must." There is so much to be offered. A survey of 120 birth moms conducted by Unplanned Good.org asked about post-placement support. The results were dismal. More than half the women said that no support was offered.[90] Yet, we could do so much to help them: Both one-on-one and group therapy and counseling should be a part of placement. Fortunately, birth mom peer support groups are now available in most major cities today, if the birth mom does the research to find and attend these groups.

We must continue to push for birth parent support, post-placement.

Read on to see some examples of the birth parent experience.

---

90 A survey of 120 birth mothers by Unplannedgood.org/

Laura's Birth Parent Story

From Burden to Blessing

In the early years of college, my voice was stolen from me in a way I didn't fully realize until later. Unable and unwilling to process the trauma in a healthy manner, I dove into my studies. As a musician, I hid in the practice room, preparing for multiple ensembles and voice lessons. I did my best to keep up appearances. I was able to graduate with two degrees, *cum laude* in four years. Next up: grad school. As the practice and study routine that I'd become accustomed to was interrupted, the trauma of my past caught up to me. I started to experience flashbacks that affected my relationships and kept me up at night.

I realized I needed to talk to someone. Through counseling, the stark realization of what happened to me was brought to light. This was a hard reality for me. I thought if I lived under the labels of "good student," "good singer," and "good girlfriend," I could keep everyone happy with me and no one would pry!

However, by 2015, those labels started to fall away, one by one. As we discussed career goals, the tension with my graduate academic advisor was unbearable. After one semester and a January term of grad school, I decided to drop out. As a side effect of the tension I felt in the Master of Music program, I no longer found joy in singing, so I stopped singing. By Memorial Day, I had broken up with my former boyfriend and jumped into another relationship the next day.

Four weeks later I had a new label, "Pregnant."

Within an hour of finding out, my "church mom" from college helped me make sense of my new reality. We both knew someone close to the family who had been struggling for years with infertility. I remember her saying, "Laura, you have two options. Knowing you, you could make a great mom. You'd figure out a way to give your child the best life possible and you'd sacrifice your own life if it came down to it. Or you could turn your burden (of this unplanned pregnancy) into a blessing for a family desperately wanting to have a child."

That phrase "burden to blessing" stuck with me.

Fast forward a few months later. In late November, after wavering between raising Henry and placing him for adoption, I finally made my decision. When I thought about raising my sweet boy, my anxiety would shoot through the roof and I started slipping into what I now know to be situational depression. However, when I thought about *adoption*, peace would wash over me.

When I was truly honest with myself, I realized I was still struggling with those events from college that had stolen my voice. I wear my emotions on my face. Kids, especially first-borns, tend to place a lot of responsibility on their shoulders that was never intended for them. So, I knew that if I kept this little boy, as we would grow together, I would have moments when I would process a difficult memory and wear the pain on my face. I hated the thought that Henry might take the blame for this. I couldn't stand it.

> ## When I thought about adoption, peace would wash over me.

You see, guilt is thinking, "I made a mistake." Shame is thinking, "I *am* a mistake."

Whereas I can deal with the guilt of my past from college, Henry has absolutely NO reason to take even an ounce of that shame on himself! Finally, when I realized I could place him into the arms of a couple eagerly wanting to start a family, a couple who were far more financially and emotionally prepared to parent, adoption was the only option left on the table.

By far, the most surprising part of this adoption journey has been how empowering it is to be a birth mom!

> ## It's surprising how empowering it is to be a birth mom.

Throughout the process, my birth mom counselor and I would text back and forth. If I said something in a text that was important, she would immediately call me and get my verbal confirmation and then follow it up with an email! Why? Because my voice was the most important one in the process and she didn't want to assume anything. In addition to that, seeing Henry's family become complete by my decision—that's empowering!

Through the process of adoption, I gained my voice back!

And now, I am a part of this beautiful sisterhood of birth moms where we celebrate, support, and grieve simultaneously with each another.

OK, enough about me. Henry is a healthy, happy, thriving six-year-old who is abounding with endless energy! Our hair has the exact same texture, which

I freak out about every time I play with it. Plus, Henry loves music just like I do! His mom sent a video of Henry cheering while watching Pavarotti sing *Nessun Dorma*! We enjoy a very open adoption where I get to see Henry and his parents about every other month, and we have a group text which keeps us all in close contact. It was clear before Henry was even born that the couple I chose to be Henry's parents were supposed to be his parents, long before I even got pregnant! Henry's parents have become some of my dearest friends and I look forward to continuing to join alongside them as we watch Henry grow!

Do I miss him? Yes. Every day.

Am I confident I made the right decision? Yes. Every day.

From burden to blessing. What was taken away from me years ago, was given back to me in a way I never could have imagined. I have regained my voice.

— Laura Blanco

Ricky's Birth Parent Story

Of two things I am certain: that my daughter loves me, and that I made the right choice. I am a birth father, and 24 years ago I chose to place my daughter, Sofie, in open adoption.

When I think back about our pregnancy and Sofie's birth, it's hard to pinpoint any singular moment in time when her birth mother and I decided that adoption was right for us. There was no "light bulb" moment, no aligning of the stars. It's complicated. It was hard for us and our families, but it was the right choice for Sofie. I am 41 years old now, and it still makes my heart race just to think back about that time in my life.

At only 16 years old, Sofie's birth mother and I were not unlike other teenage couples faced with an unplanned pregnancy. We were still going to high school, still living with our parents, still trying to discern the meaning of our lives. We were both terrified and knew we weren't capable or ready to provide this child with the stability or guidance that she deserved and needed. Heck, we were still children ourselves! I had just learned how to change the oil in my truck, and my younger sister was still only seven years old.

My parents were still raising their children. Love, however, was never a question. We both loved our precious creation and we felt the responsibility—the need even—to make sure our child was given every opportunity to succeed, to be loved and protected, and to be cherished, above all else.

It isn't that we would not have tried to raise her. We both came from loving families who would have (and do) cherish her. But we were the birth parents and we were teenagers, and teenagers make mistakes. They hurt themselves and the people around them. It's just part of growing up. I think even at the age of 16, I realized I would continue to fall on my face. Although I could accept hurting myself, I could not accept that my poor decisions might have negative impacts on Sofie's life or that I might neglect her in any way during the trials and tribulations of my teenage years. In my eyes, she was perfect and she deserved a perfect life.

At some point during the pregnancy, we began to consider open adoption. I knew if I were to forego raising her, I could only be at peace if she knew that I loved her. I still wanted to be part of her life and Sofie's mother felt the same way.

As a result, closed adoption was not an option for us. I did not want her sitting in her bedroom many years later wondering why she had blue eyes, blonde hair, braces, flat feet, and a peculiar disposition to saying "y'all" instead of "you guys." I wasn't sure how open adoption would work, but it began to take shape one day at a TGI Fridays in Houston on the faces of two wonderful people that I had never met before. That was the day I met David and Linda, Sofie's adoptive parents.

People always talk about those moments in their lives when destiny or fate makes an appearance and they "just knew it." Well, prior to that visit, I can't recall any experience where I was absolutely sure of anything, but when we met David and Linda for the first time, we just "knew it." With the exception of my own parents, there are no two people that I admire more. They have been and continue to be a blessing in my life.

> *She loves me "to the moon" and I am so grateful for that.*
> *That day in the hospital has inspired me for 24 years.*

And then came Sofie. She was perfect and amazing, and the world was too full to speak, and so was I. Her little hand grasped my pinky finger and I smelled her and I was inspired. That day in the hospital has inspired me for 24 years. Some days more than others, but never far from my heart. Sofie's birth galvanized my life in a way I could have never imagined. I finished high school and college, and I traveled. I lived in different countries and I learned a new language and how to ride horses. I married a beautiful woman. Today, I installed my very first car seat!

I wanted Sofie to be proud of me. I knew some day she would be 16 and she might wonder why I didn't raise her. I wanted to be able to say, "See, this is why I couldn't raise you. See how much I had to learn!" and I wanted it to be ok with her.

Thanks to the gracious hearts of David and Linda, I have been able to visit Sofie every year of her life and talk with her a few times a year on Christmas and birthdays. And, thanks to my mother, Sofie has always known the love of my family, even during the times when I was lost. Thanks to them, I am not a stranger, I am "Ricky," and Sofie knows my family and my wife. Someday soon, she'll meet her sister. I have always been a part of Sofie's life, but I am not her father and that's ok with me. Sofie is happy, and she is smart. I know what music she likes and that she's good at field hockey. I know her dog's name is Cody and that she loves elephants. I still get to tell her she can't date anyone until she's thirty, and that's enough for me.

Sofie is 24 years old now and she is amazing. I know she loves me because she tells me so (in texts with smiley faces). In fact, she loves me "to the moon" and I am so grateful for that. When we were expecting the birth of my second daughter, Sofie's half-sister, I'd think about Sofie's birth all the time, trying to draw parallels between the pregnancies and trying to conjure up the emotions I felt as a 16-year-old kid preparing to be a father. I am still nervous about being a father, but I am ready now.

This story would be incomplete without praising Sofie's birth mother for her bravery and sacrifice. I am so grateful to her for her selfless decision. I know how hard it was. Also, thank you to my extended family for loving Sofie as much as I do.

— Ricky

Courtney's Birth Parent story

Hi, I'm Courtney and I'm a birth mom. I'd love to share my story with you.

In high school, I was a good student—involved in extracurricular activities like choir, volunteerism, clubs, and sports. Life was great on the educational and social fronts, but my home life was another story. The parent raising me didn't like me. No, I'm not exaggerating—they just didn't like me. To counteract my home life, I started looking for love in all the wrong places, doing my best to be liked by boys. Due to this lack of self-esteem and naivete, I became pregnant in the winter of my senior year.

I was terrified. The girls at my school who had babies either suffered ridicule from other students, or dropped out after getting pregnant. I thought about the whispers behind the backs of girls who had abortions. I was paralyzed with fear over what I would do, so I called the baby's father and whispered to him that I was pregnant, hoping and praying that he would stand by me and we would make it together.

My imagination was way too generous. He ran away from the situation and from me. When I told him that I have three options—parenting, adoption, or abortion—he hung up on me. I gave him a few days and then tried to reach him again. I often joke that the term "ghosting" was created just for me. Not only did he change his pager and phone number (yeah, it was a while ago), but the baby's father actually *moved!* He literally moved to another home so that I couldn't find him. I knew that I wasn't capable of being a good parent alone, and I also knew that I didn't want to have an abortion.

Soon after, realizing I was pregnant and knowing that the father would not be there to support me, I decided to hide my pregnancy. I knew that if I told the parent with whom I lived that I was pregnant, they would make me get an abortion, so I hid the pregnancy from almost everyone. It was a lonely journey.

At this time, there was no Google, so I had to open the yellow pages to find an adoption agency nearby. I took public transportation over the December holiday break and was met by a caseworker. We talked about the entire adoption process, including the fact that I could choose my child's (adoptive) parents. We discussed the adoption laws in Georgia, the fact that I could change my mind, and a host of other topics. I had *so many questions*, but thankfully my caseworker was patient with me.

As my pregnancy progressed, my caseworker encouraged me to keep a journal of my journey, fears, and thoughts. During one meeting, I talked to the caseworker about the type of parents I hoped my child could have. At another meeting, I was able to peruse notebooks of potential adoptive parents, and I picked a couple that was absolutely perfect. They were adventurous, kind, funny, and smart. The parents I chose were everything that I thought I wasn't. See, part of the reason that I became pregnant in the first place was due to a lack of worth. My son's parents, though—oh, they were worthy!

> ### I talked to the caseworker about the type of parents I hoped my child could have.

As I mentioned earlier, it was a lonely pregnancy. I went to prenatal appointments alone, dealt with pregnancy sickness alone (it wasn't just morning sickness—I had morning, noon, afternoon, evening, and night sickness!). I hid the pregnancy as long as I could. When I couldn't hide my belly anymore, terrified, I told my parent. I was almost seven months pregnant at this point. What I feared would happen is exactly what occurred—they took me to an abortion clinic. Of course, being that far along, there was nothing that could be done, so the staff at the clinic sent me on my way.

Although it was a lonely experience, my pregnancy was amazing, even with the constant sickness! Because I made peace with my decision to choose adoption, I had to make every moment count. I would rub my belly and sing (loudly and badly) to the baby. He would kick and I would poke him right back. I cherished the weeks and months with him in my womb, because I knew it would be the only time we spent together for many years to come.

My birth story is amazing and funny at the same time. I actually didn't realize I was in labor until it was almost too late! For hours, I thought I had to use the restroom but nothing was actually happening (I'm trying not to give too much information here!). Around 10 in the morning, the pain started and that's when my brain clicked that the time had come. I was so caught off guard that I called my caseworker instead of an ambulance! She left in the middle of a meeting, picked me up, and sped me to the hospital. I can vividly remember her going through an intersection with my head out the window screaming (it's totally funny to me now).

As soon as we arrived, I was begging anyone that would listen for pain meds. Finally, a doctor told me it was way too late for that. We entered the hospital at noon and my son was born at 12:25 pm! Yes, a mere twenty-five minutes after arriving at the hospital, my son made his debut. They had to break my water on the delivery table! My caseworker held my hand throughout, and she was the first to see my son, even before I laid eyes on him.

Two days after giving birth to my beautiful boy, we left the hospital. I went home to prepare for my first day of college, and he was placed in a transitional home during the Georgia ten-day waiting period that allows birth moms to change their minds.

I went home, plopped face down on my bed, and sobbed. I mean, I cried for hours. I had such an empty feeling, literally and figuratively inside me. When I could cry no more, I cleaned my face, and came back

to reality. It was time to look into my college textbooks, figure out where my residence hall was located, and get ready to meet the stranger who would be my roommate. Just three days after placing my child into someone else's hands, I was moving into a new phase of life: adulthood and college.

A couple of months after placement, as I settled into college life, I received a phone call from my caseworker. Was I ready to meet my son's parents in person? I responded with a resounding, "Yes!"

> ## I made not only the best decision for him, but also for myself.

The four of us (my caseworker, his parents, and myself) had a fantastic dinner full of laughter and tears.

To this day, I have a souvenir from that dinner that means the entire world to me. Over the years, his parents have sent me photos and updates about *our* son, and it reminds me that I made not only the best decision for him, but also for myself. He is thriving and happy. He has had so many opportunities and blessings that I would not have been able to offer him at that time.

Recently, I was blessed to be able to see my son's mother again. Last year, we met for dinner, discussion, and laughter. I've been smiling nonstop since! On our son's 18th birthday, I went and got a tattoo of the adoption symbol placed prominently.

Overwhelmingly, I've been supported in my decision to make an adoption plan, but there have been a few Negative Nancys in my path.

"You're going to hell!" Yes, this was actually said to my face immediately after I disclosed to someone that I was choosing adoption.

"Well, you must not love your child if you can just give it away." I didn't give my child away—he's not a piece of trash. I placed my child into a loving and thriving home to give him a better chance at life. Secondly, love doesn't buy diapers. It takes much more than love to parent and raise a healthy, happy child.

> *I did not give my child away.*
> *I placed my child into a loving, thriving home*
> *to give him a better chance at life.*

I've learned that much of the negativity is due to lack of education about adoption. We just don't talk about it. Adoption was seen as a dirty secret, as something for which to be ashamed. That is why I'm so open and honest about my journey. The more that we talk about adoption, the more we can reduce the stigma.

My experience is mine; not everyone has such a positive view of adoption. For me, it's something that makes me immensely proud. Being a birth mom is not my entire identity, though it is an important part of me. I've since completed both a bachelor's and a master's degree. I've moved several times, and ended up right back here in metro Atlanta. I'm a best-selling children's book author, and I have finally realized my worth.

Choosing adoption was not easy, but it was the best decision I've ever made.

— Courtney Tierra

What Do We Learn from Birth Parents' Stories?

It's fascinating to consider the perspective of birth parents who choose to make an adoption plan. Many women who have chosen adoption do consider it the best decision they've ever made. Yes, it's inconvenient for months. And after placement, there's both healing and grieving to tackle. What a roller coaster of emotion. Intense highs and lows:

- Pain.
- Grief.
- Uncertainty.
- Anticipation.
- Sorrow.
- Relief.
- Accomplishment.
- Comfort.
- Pride.
- Satisfaction.

This is the birth mother/birth parent experience. These birth mothers have good reason to be proud of themselves. They took responsibility and intentionally made a plan that would provide for them. That's empowering!

Some people express astonishment that a woman could "give up" her baby. That might lead one to believe that she didn't love her baby. In fact, the opposite is true. The thread running through the vast majority of birth mother testimonials is this: Those women loved their babies so much that they made an adoption plan, knowing that the adoptive parents would be able to provide better for the child than the birth mother could have at that point in her life.

Most birth moms do consider their other alternatives, of course, even if briefly. If they take the time to learn about adoption, most people are surprised about how it works. Today, birth parents choose the adoptive parents. The birth mom and her partner select the couple who will parent their child. Because they can choose the parents, they also set the criteria they consider to be important—faith, careers, lifestyle, heritage, age, race, location, values. They may have a vision of the future they want for their child. And they can choose the adoptive parents who can make it happen.

The birth mom superpower is in putting her child's best interests above her own and creating the family she wants for her baby. And that's no small feat.

13

The Adoptee Perspective

"I wanted to meet [my birth mother] ... to thank her ...
She was 23 and she went through a lot to have me.
— Steve Jobs, Founder, Apple Inc.

The perspective of an adoptee is shaped by whether that adoption is open or closed. The overwhelming majority of people who were adopted in the days of closed adoptions did not have birth parents who were involved in their upbringing post-adoption. Often, the children were not told that they were adopted; some found out later, in their teens, 20s or 30s, or even later in life.

The old days of closed adoptions were entirely different from today's norm of open adoptions. These are so dissimilar they likely should not both be labeled with the same word, adoption. As a result, it's impossible to identify one big overriding theme that links adoptees' stories together over that span of time.

Now that the new standard in the US is open adoption, we are gaining insight and experience that underscores how much healthier adoption is today. The reasons why this big shift happened are to the benefit of everyone in the triad, but most assuredly, the shift to open adoption benefits birth parents and the adoptees themselves.

This is crystal clear when we read the stories of anyone who was adopted after the 1990s.

When a woman contemplates placing her baby for adoption, she will naturally wonder how things will unfold over the coming decades. The top questions a woman asks are:

- How will this child feel about my decision as he or she grows up?
- *Will my baby resent me or hate me later for placing him or her for adoption? Or will they understand?*
- Is placing the child with these parents the right thing to do?
- *How will this turn out? Will my baby have a good life? Will these parents love this child with all their hearts? Will it all be okay?*

These stories will help answer those questions.

John's Adoptee Story

My parents tried for years to conceive, with no success, and finally decided to adopt. Apparently, they were told that it would take a long time. Then, within days, they were surprised to find out that I was available, and they dropped everything to adopt me. (I will never forget asking my Dad more about this during the summer before he died, and I really enjoyed listening to my gruff father tear up as he told me the story.) Then, a few years later, once the pressure was off, they got pregnant with my younger brother. My loving, supportive parents provided me with an excellent upbringing and a happy childhood.

I always knew that I was adopted, and my family always treated it as something special. I always thought that I could have been born to anyone, but for some reason, I was placed with my family. I never, ever had any resentment towards my birth parents. I have always felt very lucky to be alive. My parents did not know much about my birth family, but one of the few things that we knew was that my birth parents were young. I imagine it would have been easy for my birth mother to terminate the pregnancy and go on with her life, but, thankfully, she chose to have me and make an adoption plan for me instead. She not only gave the incredible, selfless gift of life. She gave me a better life than she thought she could provide, and she gave my parents the most wonderful gift anyone could ever give—a family.

My parents always told me they loved me just the same as my brother, and loved me just as if I had been born to them. I always believed them, but never fully appreciated just how true that was until I had children of my own. To me, adoption is the most beautiful choice in what can be an extremely tough situation. Adoption is not perfect, it's emotionally bumpy. But as cliché as it sounds, I think adoption can be a win/win/win: It allows the mother the opportunity to relinquish the responsibility if she's not in a place to handle it. It gives the child the gift of life, and it gives two deserving people the chance to have the family of which they have dreamed. It's not easy, but everybody benefits. It's truly amazing.

I never had much desire to search for my birth parents growing up. I was content and felt lucky to have the family that I did. As I got older, my desire to learn more grew and grew. My adoptive parents have since passed away. I had been searching for my birth parents over the years since then, and ten years ago, I finally found them.

Of course, like all adoptees, I wanted to know more about my history, and wanted to see people who looked like me. But most of all, I wanted to say THANK YOU to my birth parents for the choice they made for me. They were young, and I could easily have never been born. I was truly blessed to have the opportunity to meet my birth parents and their other three children. My birth parents stayed together after I was born. They got married a couple years later and had three other children. Those children have spouses and two have children of their own. That's right, I have three full-blooded siblings, in addition to the brother with whom I grew up.

It was a little scary for all of us at the beginning, but after we worked through that, we were immediately welcomed into their family and vice versa. We visited and got to know each other over the years. Our kids always enjoy visiting their cousins, too.

Love is not a zero-sum game; it grows when you add more people. I have a whole new branch of family now, and it's wonderful. Sharing this with my wife and children has made it even more special. It has been one of the most exciting and incredible experiences, and of course one of the biggest blessings, of my entire life. I am forever grateful to them. We have basically created our own version of a grown-up, open adoption situation between my family and friends and my entire birth family!

— John Schwarz

14

The Adoptive Parent Perspective

"All that we love deeply becomes a part of us."

— Helen Keller

Whenever people comment about what a noble thing we've done by adopting my daughter, I have to smile. Most adoptive parents I know find that sentiment laughable. Adopting an infant is not noble. In many (if not most) cases, the adoptive couple wants to parent, they want to start a family, but so far, they have not been able to conceive.

Many adoptive couples have struggled with infertility for *years*—the doctor visits, the tests and X-rays, hormones, procedures, operations, the waiting followed by disappointment, month after month—*and then* spent another few *years* pursuing adoption.

Other adoptive parents have a heart for orphans and/or foster care, and have adopted older children. The "noble" label should be reserved for them. They deserve our greatest respect!

Before they can be approved to adopt a child, hopeful adoptive parents must meet high standards and complete extensive adoption screening processes.[91] Every family waiting to adopt through any reputable adoption agency has undergone several steps:

- A series of Interviews
- A financial review to ensure solvency and stability

---

91 How Adoptive Families Are Screened [3 Ways] (givingbabyupforadoption.com) https://givingbabyup foradoption.com/finding-adoptive-parents/how-are-adoptive-families-screened/

- Criminal background checks
- Medical records review
- A home inspection
- A social worker visit (or two or three)
- Securing several letters of recommendations

Of course, all of this is meant to ensure that each family, if and when they are able to adopt, will provide a safe, secure, and loving home for the baby. It assures the birth mother that she is placing her baby with a couple who is willing, ready, and able to take great care of her baby, and raise the child for the next 18+ years. Each step of this process involves more paperwork and additional third parties, which has also increased the cost of domestic adoption significantly—in fact, it has doubled in the last decade.[92]

And most adoptive parents don't mind going through those steps. If they're chosen by a birth parent and successful in adopting, they may be overwhelmed with gratitude. The privilege of raising a child born to another parent is such an honor. Most adoptive parents feel grateful, humbled, and honored to have been entrusted the role of parent: gifted with family.

---

92 https://adoptioncouncil.org/press-release/ncfa-releases-results-of-largest-study-ever-conducted-on-adoptive-parents/

Julie's Adoptive Parent Story

I used to think that if you wanted children, you could have them. Just a simple choice you made. I was vaguely aware that my parents had trouble conceiving and my grandmother had a miscarriage. I just hadn't yet experienced the complex emotions surrounding new life—both for those who didn't intend to create it, and for those who want to but can't.

I've always wanted to be a mom and experience pregnancy. And as long as I can remember, I've also had the desire to adopt a child. I think God just gave me a heart to love kids.

My husband Zach and I discussed this before we were married. We both agreed that we wanted to adopt at least one child. We assumed we would have biological children first. However, after a few years of not being able to conceive, we decided to pursue adoption instead of infertility treatments.

I feel fortunate that God gave both of us a desire to adopt. But we still had to mourn the loss of the children we couldn't have. Not just for us, but for our parents too, who had their own dreams about their grandchildren. Adopting a child would satisfy our desire to be parents, but it doesn't cure infertility.

We chose a nearby Christian agency that specializes in local/domestic adoptions. In this type of adoption, an expectant mother makes an adoption plan for her unborn baby. She has the opportunity to choose the adoptive family and determine the frequency and type of future contact she wants to have with her child.

When we began the adoption process, my heart was self-centered. I was ready to fulfill my dream of becoming a mother and bringing home a baby. Our adoption agency did an excellent job of educating and partnering with us and with the birth families throughout the process. I began to develop a deep empathy for the people on the other side of adoption: the birth family. I learned that we actually had a lot in common. Both the birth and adoptive families feel vulnerable; everyone is taking a risk and putting faith in a good outcome.

We were selected by a birth mother and had a few months to get to know her before the baby was born. It was powerful to hear why she was choosing adoption, the difficult situation she was in, and how, at that time in her life, adoption was the best way for her to care for and protect her child. I have immense compassion for this strong young woman who put the needs of her baby before her own. But it was a sweet time, too, as I got to know someone whom I really enjoy; she has a great sense of humor!

She invited me to be with her when she gave birth to a baby boy, our son Payton. When it was time to say goodbye in the hospital I cried, sobbing, as I mourned the loss that she and the other birth relatives would experience. Yet, we were also overjoyed that we were the ones chosen to be Payton's parents: Our dream of becoming a family had finally come true.

Almost two years later, another incredible young woman entrusted her preemie infant baby to us, our son Jayden. We've had fun annual visits with her and her mom over the past four years, creating great memories together. We're friends on Facebook and I also share updates and pictures. They also send gifts to the boys and call on Jayden's birthday. We are so proud that in a few months this birth mom will graduate from college.

I love both of our sons' birth mothers. They are our family now, women I care about deeply. We stay in touch with Payton's birth mom through letters. She recently wrote sweet words to us, "Hi! I miss you guys a whole lot, too. Payton has grown so much and I can hardly believe he'll be five this year! Wow. You and Zach have done a truly wonderful job with both of your boys. I am blessed to have found you both. I always feel so much joy when I receive your letters and pictures. They brighten my days."

I am in awe of how God created our family and knit our hearts together. We've been blessed with two amazing boys. We are happy that the boys have each other as brothers and friends, and that they can support each other as adoptees. All four of our parents have also completely embraced their grandsons, whom they adore and, yes, spoil.

Our sons don't look like us, but they look exactly like the children we were meant to love. It's interesting how often people tell me that we do look like each other. I guess the simplest explanation is that we do share a resemblance because we're a family.

I've been told that to experience life growing inside you is a miracle that changes you. Well, adoption is also a miracle. It changed me; it grew my heart.

Every story of becoming an adoptive parent is unique, of course. No two stories are exactly alike, yet there are also things that most adoptive parents have in common. They're willing to invest the time, energy, and money to overcome all the obstacles and meet all the challenges of successfully adopting. What drives them? Most couples who are able to adopt in this country are driven by a desire to share their love and their life with a child.

The Takeaways from These Stories

You've just heard from all parts of the triad: the birth parents who chose adoption, an adoptee, and an adoptive parent. This is open adoption today.

This small sampling reflects the consistent themes you'd find if you read dozens of these stories. Birth parents choose adoption today because they're driven by an intense love that puts a child's best interests above their own. Adoptees acknowledge that their birth moms made a difficult but loving decision to complete their pregnancies, and most appreciate knowing their stories. The transparency of open adoption makes that possible. Adoptive parents are mostly grateful for the gift of family.

These themes bear out consistently. And they are in stark contrast to the 'old days'.

As mentioned, birth moms who placed their babies in the 1960s and '70s were often pressured into adoption. Most adoptions then did not allow ongoing connection or communication. Those mothers experienced loss, sorrow, and trauma; against their will and alone. The women who delivered and relinquished their children were hurt terribly by this cruel practice.

The shift from closed to open adoption started in the 1990s and continued after 2000, and finally open adoption is quite common today. Most birth moms who place now make their own decisions, and most enter into some degree of openness. They acknowledge the extreme difficulty of the adoption decision—and also confirm that it was the right decision, not only for them, but for all involved.

Birth mothers today often feel a huge sense of accomplishment when they've completed the placement. And as time goes on, the open adoption arrangement provides continued affirmation that they made the right decision.

It's not surprising that they turn to each other for help healing, and share their stories. What may be a bit surprising is the momentum of the growing community of birth moms who share a special bond. They are posting on YouTube, writing blogs and starting podcasts to tell their stories. They are proud of themselves, and proud of each other. They want the world to know about the beauty of open adoption. And they want the world to know that women do not need to choose between abortion and parenting, because *millions* of couples are ready, willing and able to provide loving, stable homes. And finally, they want the world to know that adoption can be a positive and loving response to unplanned pregnancy.

With all that, doesn't it seem like the new paradigm of adoption warrants a fresh look?

To get adoption to the forefront of choices will require a few cultural shifts. Next, here are some segments of our society that could affect real change for the better.

PART FOUR
CALLING FOR ACTION

"Don't just bring me problems. Bring me solutions."
— Every Boss/Manager, everywhere!

15

Calling on Men to Suggest Adoption

"What makes you a man is not the ability to make a child, it's the courage to raise one."

— Barack Obama

T he first calls to action in this book call on society to be honest and more complete in discussions about the two most popular options for women facing unplanned pregnancy—single parenting and abortion. When called on to advise a woman facing unplanned pregnancy, very few people are ready, willing, or able to expose the numerous downsides of these options.

So, what will it take to get adoption on the radar? In order for adoption to get to the forefront of the choices, or at least to be considered as widely as the other two options, will require a variety of cultural shifts.

In American society today, it's very rare to hear any group proactively encourage women to consider adoption. If we could, though, what would that look like? And who is "we"?

Let's talk about the men.

In a book about adoption, should we earnestly ask men to get on board? Yes, and here's why.

Men are the #1 influencers when women facing unplanned, unwanted pregnancies need to decide on a plan. That's right, women in relationships consult with their male partners and ask for their input 74% of the time. And why not? Men *are* involved.

A new Care Net study, conducted by Lifeway Research, surveyed 1,000 American men who knew about their partner's pregnancy prior to the abortion. The study reveals that the men play a significant role in their partner's decision to have an abortion, although they may not be aware of how much influence they have.[93]

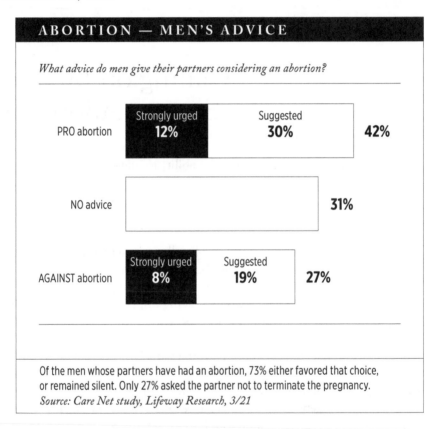

ABORTION — MEN'S ADVICE

What advice do men give their partners considering an abortion?

	Strongly urged	Suggested	
PRO abortion	12%	30%	42%
NO advice			31%
AGAINST abortion	8%	19%	27%

Of the men whose partners have had an abortion, 73% either favored that choice, or remained silent. Only 27% asked the partner not to terminate the pregnancy.
Source: Care Net study, Lifeway Research, 3/21

"In 2015, when we surveyed women who had an abortion, they indicated men were the most influential factor in their decision," said Roland Warren, president and CEO of Care Net. "Care Net recognized that despite this influence, the

---

93 https://www.baptistpress.com/resource-library/news/men-play-significant-role-in-decisions-surrounding-unplanned-pregnancies/ on a survey sponsored by Care Net, a nonprofit organization supporting more than 1,100 pregnancy centers across North America.

role of men had not yet been explored. This new study directly examines their feelings and experiences when the decision to have an abortion was made."[94]

- Nearly half (42 percent) of men whose partners had an abortion say they encouraged or strongly urged the woman to do so. In other words, almost half of the women facing unintended pregnancy followed their partners' wishes to abort. For some couples, this consultation is collaborative. In other cases, it's a high-pressure coercion that ends in abortion.[95]
- Around 3 in 10 (31 percent) say they didn't give any advice. Nearly one third of the men left the decision-making to their partner to weigh the options and make a determination about how to handle the pregnancy.
- Just imagine how different the outcomes could be if these men had suggested adoption.
- More than 1 in 4 (27 percent) say they advised or strongly urged their partner not to go through with the abortion.[96] These men advised *against* terminating the pregnancy but were unsuccessful. We don't know whether they made a constructive suggestion with an alternative plan, or whether they simply asked their partner not to end the pregnancy.

The important takeaway on that is that the men ARE involved. They do play a role in advising their partners, and can influence the outcome of the decision regarding the pregnancy.

We could be tempted to think that the reason women "need" abortions is because of incidents of rape and incest, and cases where the women's life is at risk. We hear that these are the main reasons women choose abortion. But that's not the case.

In a 2004 Guttmacher.org survey of 1,209 American women at 11 major abortion clinics, women revealed that neither health problems, nor rape, incest, or coercion by family members or partners were the primary or even secondary reasons for seeking an abortion[97] Most abortions take place because

---

94 Ibid.

95 *The National Review* recently published a column describing the prevalence of coercion, noting that 36 percent of the clients seen by the pro-life group the Human Coalition reported that someone was pressuring them to abort — that's one in three women who are pressured to end the pregnancy.

96 https://www.baptistpress.com/resource-library/news/men-play-significant-role-in-decisions-surrounding-unplanned-pregnancies/
https://www.newsbreak.com/news/2493794279293/men-play-significant-role-in-decisions-surrounding-unplanned-pregnancies
Also in https://www.kentuckytoday.com/baptist_life/men-play-significant-role-in-decisions-surrounding-unplanned-pregnancies/article_1817fe8e-7cb5-11ec-b1da-bfb6f26283c5.html

97 https://www.guttmacher.org/journals/psrh/2005/reasons-us-women-have-abortions-quantitative-and-qualitative-perspectives

the timing is inconvenient, or a child would be too expensive and/or too difficult to cope with at this time.

In addition to the inconvenience, expense, and extra challenge coping, many women feel alone—without a support system. What if the man involved could help her to know that she's not alone?

Some men push the idea of abortion because they are not ready to parent. Or they don't want to pay child support for the next 18 years. With more education about open adoption, men may come to realize that these concerns, while understandable, don't leave abortion as the only option.

The Birth Father Role

Some men advocate for abortion because they don't want to take on the financial responsibility of parenting. The new, open adoption paradigm means that they can allow the pregnancy to be completed without taking on decades of future financial obligations.

When men step up, they are in an ideal position to advocate for adoption. When they do, these men—the birth fathers—also reap all the rewards of open adoption that we've discussed, from choosing the parents to ongoing connection as the child grows.

Birth father rights differ from state to state, but most states do require the consent of the birth father if an adoption plan is being made. He can be as involved as he and his partner want. He might make a joint decision with the birth mother about their choice of adoptive parents, as Ricky did in his earlier birth father story. And he might want to stay involved in the coming few decades while the child is being raised by them.

All of this is possible.

If a man really cares about his partner's mental and physical health—both in the short term and the long term—as well as the health of her (or their) future babies, he might have second thoughts about suggesting abortion, if only he had complete information on all the options. If they're not ready to parent, he might just become an advocate of adoption. He might advocate for adoption for some of the same reasons a woman would choose it: wanting a life for their child that is more, and better, than what they can provide at the time.

16

Calling on Churches to Meet People Where They Are

"Let us have faith that right makes right, and in that faith let us, to the end, dare to do our duty as we understand it."

— Abraham Lincoln

The positive impact of religious institutions—as they have utterly transformed societies across the world since the days of Jesus Christ 2,000 years ago—cannot be overstated. Throughout history, churches have founded schools, hospitals and orphanages. Christians have campaigned for prison reform and better housing, helped to establish a huge number of charities to support the poor, the underprivileged, prisoners and their families, the homeless, and those seeking justice. It was Christian initiative that put an end to the slave trade in the US and ended apartheid in South Africa. On any given day, the church makes a difference to millions of lives across the world.[98]

It's often said that we must meet people where they are in life. In this case, that means pregnant and scared. But, once a woman is pregnant, our communities of faith are often silent. Or worse, she is met with judgment, shamed, cast out.

Many in our faith communities had been praying for the overturn of the Roe decision. That has happened, now what? It's time to seize the opportunity to step up, step in, and help women. Communities of faith could engage with,

---

98 https://christianity.org.uk/article/good-done-by-the-church

assist, and empower women facing unplanned pregnancy, if we meet people where they are, and move forward from there.

Adoption is a brave, loving, positive decision that any person of genuine faith can support. And women from all different faiths do choose adoption for their babies.

- Compassion and placing the needs of others above our own are core values of the Christian faith. Adoption not only embodies these concepts, our adoption into the Kingdom of God is a core belief. We also believe that God can use anyone to accomplish great things. True here, too.
- The Islamic view of adoption can vary with where you live. Some Islamic nations have cultural standards that don't embrace adoption. In the West, however, there are more accepting views of a pregnant Muslim woman choosing adoption. Caring for the "orphan" is a clear Islamic doctrine. Preference would be to place with family, but open adoption practices in the US today make it possible for a Muslim birth mother to find, and place with, a Muslim family.
- Jewish tradition is full of stories that support adoption. In an early example, Moses' mother, Miriam, chose to do what was best for him by leaving him in the care of Pharoah in Egypt. Some Orthodox communities do not embrace the idea of placing a baby outside of the community. However, most Conservative and Reform Jewish communities not only support adoption, in many cases they also celebrate placement of the baby as a mitzvah.
- Eastern religions also have positive adoption stories. The Buddha himself actually "gave up" his child in pursuit of enlightenment. He left his son to fulfill his purpose in this life but first ensured that his son would be well-loved and cared for.[99]

In theory, communities of faith do accept adoption and embrace historical examples. In practice, we have a ways to go.

All too often, women with unexpected pregnancies go silently from their place of worship to the abortion clinic, convinced their religion would condemn and/or shame them. More than four in ten women who've had an abortion belonged to a religious community when they ended a pregnancy, and only seven percent of women discussed their abortion decision with anyone

---

99 https://givingbabyupforadoption.com/what-is-adoption/can-you-put-baby-up-adoption
/religious-views-on-giving-child-up-for-adoption/

there, according to the researchers who conducted the survey discussed in the prior section.[100] Among women who have had an abortion:

- Three-fourths (76 percent) say their church had no influence on their decision to end a pregnancy.
- Two-thirds (65 percent) say church members judge single women who are pregnant.
- A majority (54 percent) think churches oversimplify decisions about pregnancy options.
- Fewer than half (41 percent) believe churches are prepared to help with decisions about unwanted pregnancies.
- Only three in ten think churches give accurate advice about pregnancy options.[101]

Many facing the prospect of discussing their pregnancy with members of their religious community shudder to think of the reaction they would face if they were to darken the threshold of a house of worship while single and visibly pregnant. It's been said, "I'd much rather ask for forgiveness than help." That's because of the shame they feel. The faith community could change this NOW. All we have to do is remember that we are not here to judge. Let he who is without sin cast the first stone. (John 8:7)

> ## "I'd much rather ask for forgiveness than help."

Shame on us, if shaming the young pregnant woman is our first response. Instead, we are called to embrace these women without judgment. We can show compassion and love. This is an opportunity for any denomination to model the qualities we hope to instill in our children. Some religious groups already fund, and even staff, their community's local Crisis Pregnancy Center. Some are now stepping up to help. They're leveraging their authority and position to take up the role of supporter, encourager, and empowerer. Be aware of

---

100 IBID.
101 https://www.baptistpress.com/resource-library/news/men-play-significant-role-in-decisions
-surrounding-unplanned-pregnancies/
https://www.newsbreak.com/news/2493794279293/men-play-significant-role-in-decisions
-surrounding-unplanned-pregnancies
Also in
https://www.kentuckytoday.com/baptist_life/men-play-significant-role-in-decisions-surrounding
-unplanned-pregnancies/article_1817fe8e-7cb5-11ec-b1da-bfb6f26283c5.html

all the resources in your local community, so that these women are supported with assistance, education, and affirmation.

This is the time to lead! There is a huge opportunity for communities of faith to have a positive impact. Religious leaders often serve as spiritual counselors and trusted advisors. In those roles, they could help pregnant women, unwilling or unable to parent, see that she has another option.

Religious congregations could step in and embrace these women, truly help them understand their choices and the long-term effects of each option. Communities of faith could make a huge difference.

When a woman realizes she's pregnant, embrace the opportunity to start a dialogue. Move forward with comprehensive information, plentiful encouragement, and practical assistance. Empathize, comfort, assist, pray for and provide for the woman who chooses to complete her pregnancy and place her baby with a loving family.

Be there for her.

17

Calling on Corporate America:
Advance Positive Options

"You're Always One Choice Away from Changing Your Life"
— Mac Anderson

Companies offer employees certain benefits when they become parents. These are typically thought about with regard to parenting biological children or adoptive children.

Adoptive parents are covered by federal law: The Family and Medical Leave Act (FMLA) provides eligible employees up to 12 workweeks of unpaid leave a year. Family leave benefits, for both new moms and new dads, are now offered routinely, and many states supplement those benefits. Employees can add on sick pay, paid time off, and even short-term disability to stretch their time at home after a newborn arrives. Insurance covers hospital stays: Health Savings Accounts (HSAs) cover a plethora of other expenses.

Since the Small Business Job Protection Act of 1996, adoption tax credits help with some of the cost to adopt. The IRS grants a tax credit of $14,890 to families that incur adoption-related expenses in 2022.[102] These include legal fees, court costs, and travel expenses. The nearly $15K in tax credits that adoptive couples can receive from the federal government doesn't come close to covering the entire cost of an adoption these days. Sometimes employers help

---

102 Taxpayers should complete Form 8839, Qualified Adoption Expenses.

with this as well: The most comprehensive employee benefits packages include some amount of adoption expense reimbursement.

Since the Supreme Court overturned the Roe decision in 2022, numerous larger corporations have added generous "abortion coverage" to their employee benefits packages. According to the Society for Human Resource Management (SHRM), employers are covering not only the procedure itself, but also the travel to and from states in which abortion is legal at their stage of pregnancy—for both the employee and her covered spouse/partner.[103] Furthermore, "under the newly announced abortion-travel benefits, employers promise a cash benefit to formerly pregnant employees who return from travel no longer pregnant due to abortion."[104]

What about Birth Parent Benefits?

Most of the adoption benefits offered by companies to their employees today are meant to assist adoptive parents. It's interesting to look at the employee benefits packages from the viewpoint of the birth parent who chooses adoption. Companies today must offer the same benefits to women who choose adoption after delivery of their babies. They are entitled to those same FLMA benefits—12 weeks of unpaid leave. Since most birthmothers are single, the lack of paid leave could very well be a hardship. The birth mother may not be able to take the time off if she has to forgo her pay during her leave.

If companies wanted to be adoption-friendly, they would do better.

Here is an example of one company doing just that: Peter Rex is the founder and CEO of REX, a set of companies that solve pain points in owning and operating real estate. In a *Newsweek* magazine opinion piece, the CEO comments:

> *"The typical business argument in favor of abortion comes down to productivity. A comprehensive review of relevant studies in 2018 found that both pro-life and pro-abortion researchers agree that "abortion is consistently associated with elevated rates of mental illness" and "the abortion experience directly contributes to mental health problems for at least some women." These findings are tough to square with the standard corporate argument. If there's a way to help employees avoid mental health issues, companies should take it. . . .*

---

103 https://www.shrm.org/resourcesandtools/hr-topics/benefits/pages/companies-announce-abortion
-travel-benefits-following-dobbs-decision.aspx
104 https://eppc.org/publication/big-companies-should-think-twice-about-abortion-benefits/

Companies like Apple and Amazon were founded by people who were the result of unplanned pregnancies. Fortunately, Steve Jobs and Jeff Bezos entered the world—and transformed it. If for no other reason than pure self-interest, companies should want to expand the pool of human potential, not shrink it."[105]

He recently announced that his business offers $7,500 to employees who want to have their baby and place the child for adoption. REX is one of the *only* companies to offer any assistance to the employee who becomes a birth parent and chooses adoption. This corporate support for the adoption option is shockingly rare. Given all the financial support offered by corporate America to promote abortion, why is there no corresponding policy to promote adoption? There should be.

> ## Companies today are simply not offering needed benefits to birth mothers who choose adoption.

Rex continues.

"Doing so would send a message of inclusion and empowerment to employees who may want to continue their pregnancy but need some extra support. . . . Supporting adoption is good for business, in the short and long term. That fact alone should be enough to convince corporate America to throw its financial weight behind helping pregnant team members choose life."[106]

What if corporate America were to encourage adoption? What could that look like? What about possibly offering "pregnancy leave" to cover the last trimester and/or the first few months after giving birth and placing the baby with an adoptive couple? Or a more liberal work-from-home policy? Maybe a clothing allowance? Maybe tuition reimbursement for the birth mother who starts college or night classes after placement? What about covering gym memberships and other needs the woman may have after she places her baby for adoption?

Let's take better care of our female employees.

We've learned so much about the unintended outcomes of both abortion and single parenting. Let's support women as they try to avoid the life-long side

---

105 https://www.newsweek.com/companies-should-support-adoption-not-abortion-opinion-1723563
    July 13, 2022
106 https://www.newsweek.com/companies-should-support-adoption-not-abortion-opinion-1723563
    July 13, 2022

effects of the binary choice. We know so much now about how to do adoption well. The big picture, with complete information, must include adoption.

> *Supporting adoption is good for business, in the short and long term, because it's better for women's health.*

The cultural shift to support adoption could become a reality if more companies had the courage to lead. Let's challenge corporate America to step up, to step in, and provide equal emphasis on adoption as an option for women facing unplanned pregnancy.

What's in it for the corporation? A lot! For the birth mother, for the adoptive couple she chooses, and for the child. That child will grow up to become a valued employee *somewhere*.

18

Calling on the Medical Community to Lead on the Front Lines

"First, do no harm."

— The ancient Greek Physician Hippocrates

Obstetricians and gynecologists (OB/GYNs) are often the front line for pregnant women. If a woman is visiting her doctor for a pregnancy test, once the pregnancy is confirmed, the next words out of the doctor's mouth are critical.

That used to be, "Congratulations! You're expecting!"

Now, the doctor might say, "You're pregnant. How do you feel about that?"

Or they might even say, "You're pregnant. Do you want to keep it?"

Each of these three statements is a reflection of our shifting culture—yesterday and today.

In that first conversation, the woman is forming her thoughts about the news, and her options. If that first discussion includes only the two default options, it's much harder to get adoption on the table after the fact.

To help shed light on doctor responsibilities and opportunities with respect to unplanned pregnancy options, I interviewed Donna Harrison M.D., *Chief Executive Officer of AAPLOG.*

I asked Dr. Harrison more about the work they do. Here's an excerpt of our interview.

Question: What is the AAPLOG message for the public? What is it that you want people to know?

Answer: AAPLOG exists to make known the effects of abortion on both of our patients, the pregnant woman and her preborn child. Elective abortion hurts both. We communicate this reality at every opportunity in the legal, policy, and public arenas.

Q: What about on the individual level, when a woman learns she's pregnant?

A: As physicians who specialize in reproductive health, we know that women are empowered by accurate information. The abortion industry often does not talk with women about the serious risks to a woman's physical and mental health associated with abortion. As physicians we believe that the truth about all options should be discussed with the patient.

Q: Regarding the major/main consequences of abortion, as I read in Dr Francis' *Newsweek* article, *Doublespeak*, you say that "Many women undergo [abortion] procedures without knowing the long-term costs to their own health and the health of their future children. Why is that not more widely known? What are you doing to educate the public about that?"

A: Unfortunately, many major medical organizations are acting as pro-abortion activists, rather than as physicians. We have a coordinated media outreach that talks about the harms of abortion to women.

Q: Our society tells us that abortion is fast, easy, acceptable. No problem. No worries. Yet you say that "Elective abortions can exact an immense physical and emotional toll on women later in life." Tell me more about that.

A: There's a large number of studies documented in our Practice Bulletins and Committee Opinions. Here are a few areas explored and reports on the links between:

- Abortion and the long-term Effects on Mental Health:
- https://aaplog.org/wp-content/uploads/2019/12/FINAL-Abortion-Mental-Health-PB7.pdf
- Abortion and (future) Preterm Births:
- https://aaplog.org/wp-content/uploads/2021/11/PB-5-Overview-of-Abortion-and-PTB.pdf
- Abortion and Breast Cancer:
- https://aaplog.org/wp-content/uploads/2020/01/FINAL-CO-8-Abortion-Breast-Cancer-1.9.20.pdf

Q: "Preterm births" don't sound too serious to me. How does that result in 3 million infant deaths worldwide each year?

A: Abortion increases the risk of VERY preterm births, that is babies born between 22 and 26 weeks, at the edge of life. These little babies struggle to breathe and have to have neonatal intensive care support to survive. Many of the 22–24-week-old babies don't survive.

Q: Once a woman is facing a pregnancy that's not planned, for which of the three options do you advocate?

A: As physicians who counsel women in that situation, the practice of 'informed consent' requires that we discuss all options with the patient.

Q: In our society, whose responsibility is it to advocate more for adoption? Adoption agencies can be seen as predatory with this message. Most churches don't get involved. Who should take up this fight?

A: It's a great question. I think personally that there needs to be more success stories about adoption. There are many excellent examples of adoption success stories. These successes need to become part of an overall messaging and storytelling about adoption.

Maybe more OB/GYNs could re-think their first words to their patients after telling a woman she's pregnant. Maybe more successful adoption stories will eventually dispel the myths of the old days and inform people about the beauty of adoption today. Maybe more doctors could keep this option top of mind and be ready to advocate with encouraging words and comprehensive lists of local resources for pregnant women.

In the name of "informed consent," more information about both the short- and long-term physical and mental health effects of abortion should be shared with women before they opt for the procedure.

And, in the medical community, more (bipartisan) research on short- and long-term health outcomes after abortion should be a higher priority.

19

Calling on (Grand)Parents & Educators to Suggest Adoption

"All great change in America begins at the dinner table."
— President Ronald Reagan's Farewell Speech
from the Oval Office 1/11/89

When women face unplanned pregnancy, the very first resource one might wish for them is a loving, caring adult who can review all their options with them.

Parents and Grandparents

If your defiant child wants to discount your parental advice, they shout, "Why should I listen to *you*, anyway??" One favorite answer is, "Because I love you more than anyone else on the planet. That's why."

Our kids' social groups don't have their best long-term interests at heart. But children forget that when they succumb to the power of peer pressure.

If you are a parent (or a grandparent!), you have a greater influence on your teen's decision-making (particularly about sex) than you may realize. And today, your teen needs you more than ever. What you might not expect: adolescents actually want their parents to talk about sex. Typically, adolescents (both older and younger teens) identify their parents as being most influential in terms of their decisions regarding sex.[107]

Children DO listen to their parents more than we think. Talking to your teen works—and it makes a big difference. Fathers: This includes you, too! In the case of teen moms, it is often the grandparents' perspective that drives the outcome.

That's why it's extremely important that we as parents or grandparents step into that role and lead. We need to model critical thinking and teach our kids how to be accountable for their actions. How to make their own decisions. How to evaluate alternatives. How to balance short-term and long-term impact.

Here's a fact: Three in ten American girls will get pregnant before age 20. That is almost 750,000 pregnancies a year.[108] Once that happens, what's your response? Of course, you'll want to help them evaluate their options. You may want to think about your advice in advance. Now that you know about the long-term outcomes associated with both abortion and single parenting, you may want to recommend adoption. You might consider it to be in your daughter's best interests.

Maybe, like many, you just haven't thought about it. But the more one learns about open adoption today, the more one is inclined to recommend adoption. Many women choose adoption because they want to give their baby the best possible chance at life, and adoption gives them the chance to watch their baby grow up happy and healthy. Later in life, they can be proud of this decision, and the relationship with their adult son or daughter can be extremely satisfying and rewarding.

With all that, you might just become a big fan of the idea.

Educators

Much of the above information in this chapter applies to your child's favorite teacher as much as it applies to parents. Some have advised that this section should not include educators, since that could be quite controversial. However, many (if not most) public schools have turned over their freshman year biology class to their local Planned Parenthood to conduct a full week of sex ed. There, your children are told that "everyone's doing it," meaning having sex. (So, what's wrong with you if you're not??) Often, the sex ed class

---

107 https://powertodecide.org/news/how-parents-shape-teens-sexual-decision-making-for-better
108 *www.dosomething.org.* April 20, 2016.

presents abortion and (single) parenting as the logical answers to unplanned pregnancy. Adoption is not included as one of those potential answers.

In high school, and even junior high school, we can encourage people to advocate for adoption. We can remind them of the false dilemma: it's not a choice between abortion and parenting. There *is* another option. All it takes sometimes is for an adult who's in the right place at the right time to seize the opportunity and highlight the benefits of adoption.

What a difference a suggestion can make! The one study done on this topic shows that women facing unplanned pregnancy are 50% more likely to choose adoption if a mentor or other adult figure in their life suggests it.[109] Not in a flippant, under-the-breath kind of way, but as a serious idea for thoughtful consideration.

Your suggestion could make ALL the difference!

---

109 https://infantadoptionguide.com/adoption-as-an-option-for-women-facing-unplanned-pregnancy-with-unplannedgood-org-podcast-episode-76/

20

Calling for True Sisterhood

"To love is to will the good of another."

— Thomas Aquinas

Anyone raised with siblings knows this scenario: *"I can tease my sister, steal her makeup, and short sheet her bed. I can do all that. But if YOU hurt my sister, I'll deck ya!"*

We need and love our sisters. There are many aspects of a woman's life that only another woman can understand. Our ability to empathize with, and show compassion for, each other is unequalled.

Women with a strong supportive group of female friends have greater chances of thriving than women who are socially isolated. It is through sisterhood that we nurture and enjoy the fruits of friendship, giving and receiving emotional support.

We do better when we belong, when we are in community. Women actually crave deep emotional connections. We get these with our sisters, both blood sisters and chosen "sisters." That's what we're wired for: community and connection.

We also expect, rightly, that our sisters will fire a warning shot if we are heading toward a cliff. If they see danger ahead, or we're making poor choices, we expect them to say something. And usually, they do.

This beautiful concept of community means looking out for each other, having each other's back. But somewhere along the way, we seem to have lost that as we place an ever-higher value on the individual. In a world that talks nonstop about our personal "rights," it's tempting to cling to that "all about me" mindset. And in doing so, we confuse the choices others might make with a perceived violation of our "rights." We mistake and obscure what we would choose with what we think others should choose. At the same time, the greater good—what's best for the collective community—falls far from focus.

Let's remind ourselves what the community of sisterhood looks like. And what it *feels* like.

Inside of that circle, we understand each other, hear each other, love each other. That love drives our relationships. The power of sisterhood is never more deeply felt than when we're helping another down her own path, not telling her what her path should be.

We are not alone. We're stronger together. We're healthier. We are loved.

One definition for loving someone is that you care more about their well-being than your own. This is what drives a woman to be a part of a community. It's also what drives a woman to choose adoption: the superpower of a birth mom is her ability to think beyond herself for the good of another. She wants to know that her child will be provided for better than she is able to do at this time, even though there's a cost to her for making this choice.

> **Love means caring more about another's well-being than your own. This is the super power of a birth mother.**

So why, in the case of unplanned, unwanted pregnancy, does the community of sisterhood suddenly fall apart? It's time to resume the role of the good sister. Time to be a true friend again and watch out for each other. The first step toward that is honesty. When one of our sisters is in a dilemma and comes to us for advice, let's start by providing complete information. Step up and share the truth about all the options.

For very good reason, we've embraced a new adoption paradigm in this country. When we look clearly, we can see several silver linings: Choosing adoption is not only choosing life for your child, and choosing parents for your child, but also creating the possibility of a life-time relationship with the child and his/her adoptive family, which YOU helped create.

Encourage your "sister" to think about it. Help her to weigh her options and what's really in her best interests, both short term and long term. Adoption is an option worth serious consideration—and it might just be the best option. Show her these stories of birth mothers and birth fathers who chose adoption.

They are honest and raw about how hard it was to choose adoption, AND the vast majority describe it as the greatest accomplishment of their lives.

Show that you've got the back of the woman you love. Help her understand what open adoption is today.

Conclusion

We are breaking records these days in the US!

The USA has the highest rate of unplanned pregnancy among all Western countries. Specifically, teen pregnancy in the USA is the highest in the industrial world. At the same time, about two million couples are waiting to adopt.[110] That's millions of couples hoping to provide a loving home life where a child would thrive. Yet, only about one percent of American women facing unplanned pregnancy choose adoption. Open adoption is simply not on the radar when we counsel women facing an unwanted pregnancy.

Clearly, it's time to re-examine how we respond to unplanned pregnancy in the US.

When we're honest, we can admit that all three options have impact that lasts a lifetime. All three options also have significant downsides – some in the short-term, some in the long-term, or both.

Adoption. It's worth reconsidering. So much good can come from an unplanned pregnancy when women choose open adoption. The way open adoption works today ideally keeps the child's best interests at the forefront.

No, it won't be easy. But with adoption, there can also be great beauty, immeasurable reward, and bountiful family—more lives filled with more love. Hopefully the stories in this book have shown that.

Suggest open adoption to a woman you love, for her own sake. As she turns to you and gives you the opportunity to advise her, do so with complete information. Walk alongside her, and offer her the resources, support and encouragement she needs to make a good decision—in the big picture.

---

110 Vital and Health Statistics Series 23, Number 27 (August 2008) (cdc.gov)
https://www.cdc.gov/nchs/data/series/sr_23/sr23_027.pdf Page 24, Series 23, No. 27

When the woman you love suddenly faces an unplanned pregnancy she may seek your advice. She'll need to make a decision. Will you step aside while she listens to current culture tell her there are only two options? Will you remain silent while she chooses, unknowingly, to risk her health? Or will you step up and encourage her to consider adoption, potentially giving her the opportunity to create a family and forever take pride in herself and her accomplishment.

We'll never know, though, unless YOU suggest it.

It's time for a loving, positive response to unplanned pregnancy.

Afterword.
A Birth Mother's Reflections

The story of one birth mother, Ali, opened this book, telling us about her unplanned pregnancy and why she chose adoption for her baby. Now, a decade later, and with the benefit of hindsight, Ali adds to her story.

I'll never forget the moment when I told my delivery nurse that my daughter would be placed for adoption and that her adoptive parents were sitting in the waiting room with my father. In her over ten years of being a nurse, she had never, knowingly, been a part of a birth mother's adoption journey. She sat with me and flipped through their adoption profile as I answered questions and spoke about how grateful I was to have found them and formed the relationships I have with them. A day after delivering my sweet Olivia, she was off work, but came by to introduce me to her own son and thank me for opening up to her about my story and reasons for choosing adoption. She didn't know birth mothers could have the amount of control that I had in making my decision for my daughter.

The "pro-adoption movement" is something I didn't even know existed until a year or so after becoming a birth mother. That first year, I chose to continue to get to know my daughter and her parents, while reflecting on, and for the most part, remaining silent about my adoption journey outside of my family and closest friends. Not because of shame, but because even within my own personal family, there were pointed questions that, while asked out of love, were simply coming from a place of misunderstanding.

Now, I look back at the early experiences and conversations of my adoption journey, and realize not only how much I myself have learned, but how my story has inadvertently helped those around me—of all ages, backgrounds, professions, and cultures—realize how far adoption has come. Those early, intimate conversations with people I love are what really pushed me to want to publicly share my story and join the pro-adoption movement in 2015.

I'm glad I felt confident enough to start sharing this publicly, because it allowed me to meet everyone from fellow birth mothers from whom I've learned, to true pro-adoption champions-turned-friends—all of whom continue to motivate and inspire me each and every day.

This has given me a platform and the ability to help other girls and women from all different backgrounds who are struggling with unplanned pregnancy. I am able to share my story and reassure other birth parents that you will make it through this journey and in the end everything will be okay.

When Terri reached out, asking if my story could be included in the book she was writing, I was humbled and honored. Not only because it would allow my story to continue to be heard and potentially help other birth mothers, but also because after getting to know Terri, I know how many people she has impacted through her 14 years in the adoption community—thanks to her non-judgmental heart for adoption.

I am honored to contribute to Pro-Choice, Pro-Adoption. It's Time for a Loving, Positive Response to Unplanned Pregnancy. I'm excited for those who read it to learn about and have a better understanding of open adoption, so they can help women experiencing unplanned pregnancies just like me know that adoption is a beautiful, third choice.

– Ali Marie Watson

Resources

There are numerous resources, clinics & organizations available to help. The following pages include just a small sample to get you started. Many sources of information and practical assistance are available.

INTRODUCTION TO CARE RESOURCES

There are three kinds of Women's Clinics:

1) Medical care clinics / pregnancy centers that provide a full spectrum of health care for women, but not abortions,
2) Clinics that mainly provide abortions plus a few selected reproductive care services like STD testing and birth control,
3) Federal Qualified Health Centers that provide comprehensive care to vulnerable populations and some women's health services.

1) Fully licensed, community-funded, **women's medical care clinics** provide professional consultations, well-woman care (annual exams including breast exams and mammogram referrals), pregnancy testing, ultrasounds (to determine viability and pregnancy dating), STD/STI testing and treatment, pre-abortion screenings, abortion education, abortion pill reversal, prenatal care, childbirth classes, pregnancy loss healing, health education, & referrals for both men and women. Many of these also provide practical support items such as: diapers, formula, baby supplies such as car seats, clothes and carriers. Board-certified medical

professionals—OB/GYN physicians, registered nurses, nurse practitioners, medical assistants, and support staff—are dedicated to providing quality, holistic medical care. Pregnancy centers are typically privately funded and focused on supporting pregnant women facing difficult circumstances with medical care and referrals, education, mentoring, and material support at virtually no cost to the client. Usually, services are provided at no-cost to low-cost (sliding fee scale) and will bill Medicaid and some private insurance. These are numerous and outnumber abortion clinics by about 14:1 so they are accessible across the Country.

2) The **abortion clinics** mainly provide abortions as their core business. Most offer selected reproductive care services like STD testing and birth control, and sometimes breast exams. Usually, service fees are charged on a sliding scale. They do not offer their patients ultrasounds outside of the abortion procedure or for patient viewing. Most do not offer prenatal care. They do not offer mammograms.

3) **Federal Qualified Health Centers** Federally funded health clinics provide comprehensive care and women's health services to vulnerable and underserved populations on a sliding scale. They offer services to all, regardless of a person's ability to pay. These health centers' services include behavioral health, primary care, chronic care management, preventive care and other services such as radiology, laboratory services, dental care, transportation, translation and social services. Federally Qualified Health Centers (FQHC) receive funds from the HRSA Health Center Program. https://findahealthcenter.hrsa.gov/ https://www.definitivehc.com/blog/how-many-fqhcs-are-there

Medical care clinics / pregnancy centers (2) and FQHC sites (3) are not dependent on abortion for revenue, and instead offer women holistic care.

Once you've decided which kind of clinic you want, they are easy to find in an online search.

The Lozier Institute did research on the number of each kind of clinic and updated their data in July 2022. There are:

- **5300+ Federal Qualified Health Centers (FQHCs),**
- **2700 Medical care clinics / pregnancy centers,**
- **585 Planned Parenthood locations in the USA,**
  https://lozierinstitute.org/realchoices/#quick-facts

Surprising outcome:

There are 14 comprehensive care clinics and women's medical health centers for **every** Planned Parenthood location. https://lozierinstitute.org/health-clinics-nationwide-compared-to-planned-parenthood-centers/

CARE FOR PREGNANT WOMEN

Medical Clinics

- **Obria (& Obria Affiliate) Medical Clinics,** https://obria.org/ Fully licensed community care clinics provide professional medical consultations, well-woman care, pregnancy testing, ultrasounds, STD/STI testing and treatment, pre-abortion screenings, abortion education, abortion pill reversal, prenatal care, health education and referrals. Our board-certified OB/GYN physicians, registered nurses, nurse practitioners, medical assistants - all highly trained and dedicated to meeting your health care needs – are on staff. https://locator.obria.org/ and https://obria.org/affiliate/
- Care Net https://www.care-net.org/ Serving 1200+ affiliated pregnancy centers in the US with 30,000 volunteers, Care Net provides immediate support and a range of free services to women and men facing unplanned pregnancy. Abortion Information, Adoption Information, Housing Referrals, Maternity & Infant Supplies, Medical Referrals, Parenting Education, Post-Abortion Support, Pregnancy Options Information, Pregnancy Tests, STD/STI Information, STD/STI Tests, STD/STI Treatment, Support for Men, Ultrasound (Mobile), Ultrasound (Onsite), Ultrasound Referrals. Go to https://www.care-net.org/.
- **Save the Storks.** savethestorks.com Visit a mobile pregnancy clinic at one of 80 stork busses in 30 states across the US. These mobile pregnancy centers offer compassion, education and holistic care, plus free support and medical care including pregnancy tests and counseling, ultrasounds, STI testing, parenting and prenatal education programs, after-abortion support and material resources. Find the bus near you: https://savethestorks.com/what-we-do/stork-bus-locations/

The clinics that do not offer abortions are community-funded, grassroots organizations, whereas the abortion facilities are increasingly funded by taxpayer dollars. Nevertheless, these clinics abound. A quick online search will lead you to either in your town, or nearby.

Clinic Resources

Heartbeat International is a resource hub for the above pregnancy care service organizations. Through their affiliate network, they provide training and continuous learning, resources for those in the pregnancy help community, education for more than 6,500 women and men each year, and professional and compassionate care for women and men in need. **Option Line, 24/7 helpline (1-800-712-HELP)** To find a Heartbeat affiliate, start here: https://www.heartbeatinternational.org/services-home

OTHER WOMEN'S HEALTH RESOURCES

Mammograms & Ultrasounds

Many of these health care clinics offer cancer screenings including mammograms and ultrasounds. The U.S. Food and Drug Administration (FDA) reports that there are 8,735 licensed mammography facilities in America (Note that Planned Parenthood operates none of them). The FDA has a search engine here to find a mammogram resource near you: https://www.accessdata.fda.gov/scripts/cdrh/cfdocs/cfMQSA/mqsa.cfm

Free Phone Counseling

- Care Net. Call 877-791-5475
- Gladney Center for Adoption. Text or call 1-800-236-7896
- Lifeline Children's Services. Call or Text: 1.800.875.5595
- **LifeTime Adoptions. Call** or **text 1-800-923-6784** 24/7
- Pregnancy Decision Line. Call 866-925-4610 or 866-802-4705 Heartbeat International - Option Line, 24/7 helpline (1-800-712-HELP)

Support For Single Moms

- **The Life of a Single Mom** is a national nonprofit that exists to see that no single mom walks alone. The organization works with churches and community partners to start single mom's support groups in cities throughout the U.S. The group offers a Single Mom Support Group Curriculum, Single Mom University, Single Mom Support Group

Start-Up Packages & workbook, One-on-One Coaching **...and much more!** https://thelifeofasinglemom.com/
- **LoveLine** Providing comprehensive case management for pregnant or single moms. "Choosing between her baby and her bills should not be an option." Loveline is a crisis call line for women facing unplanned pregnancies who feel they have exhausted resources in their area. Our hope is to discover the need, uncover hidden resources and connect her with one of our volunteer advocates in her area to help. LoveLine will be accessible 24/7/365.
- **Mama Scholar** is a project in collaboration with Embrace Grace to offer young unwed mothers the opportunity to complete their education by awarding scholarships to mothers who complete the Embrace Grace program. https://mamascholar.com/
- **ProLove Ministries** ProLove Ministries connects resources so that anyone facing problems or crisis situations regardless of stage of development, race, age, gender, or ability will have a network of solutions that help instead of harm. https://proloveministries.org/
- **Safe Haven Laws.** Every state in the USA has Safe Haven Laws so that any mother can relinquish her baby at safe, designated places, no questions asked!
- **Second Mothers.org for foster and adoptive moms.**
  - Prevention. Keeping children with their mothers.
  - Intervention. Helping women and vulnerable children in crisis.
  - Restoration. Supporting foster and adoptive mothers.

See private Facebook group at https://www.facebook.com/groups/secondmother
See Second Mothers Bible Study on Amazon.

ADOPTION RESOURCES

Adoption Agencies.

Find an agency you trust. Work with them to identify the hopeful adoptive couples who might be a match for you. As you make an adoption plan, remember that YOU make the decisions: who you choose to parent your baby can **reflect your values.** You choose their faith, two-career couple or stay-at-home mom, younger or more established, rural or urban, other siblings or not, ideas on education, and much more.

Please see BraveLove.org for a Directory of Recommended Adoption Agencies.

Please see InfantAdoptionGuide.com for helpful tips & resources in choosing an Adoption agency.

NOTE: Even if you are not sure you want to place for adoption, these agencies can offer information, practical assistance and other resources.

FIND an ADOPTION AGENCY is a step-by-step through the entire process of finding and choosing a trusted, ethical agency. https://www.find-myadoptionagency.com/ Here are some of the national adoption agencies, though not a complete list.

- Abrazo Adoption Assoc. https://abrazo.org/ 800-454-5683
- American Adoptions http://www.americanadoptions.com/ (800) 236-7846
- Angel Adoption, Inc. www.angeladoptioninc.com 847-462-8874
- Bethany Christian Services Bethany.org or https://impregnant.org/ adoption (844) 838-4269
- Christian Adoptions Alliance https://christianadoptions.org/ Search agencies by state.
- Hand in Hand Adoptions https://handinhandadoption.org (831) 438-3736
- Lifetime Adoption https://lifetimeadoption.com (800) 923-6784
- Nightlight Christian Adoptions https://www.nightlight.org/ (502) 423-5780 For more info, including chat counseling, visit http://mypregnancymyfuture.org

Funding: Adoption Grants, Loans and Information

- Fund your Adoption TV fundyouradoption.tv
- Lifesong for Orphans, lifesong.org
- Show Hope, showhope.org
- ABBA Fund, abbafund.org
- Pathways for Little Feet, pathwaysforlittlefeet.org
- JSC Foundation, jscfoundation.org
- A Child Waits Foundation, achildwaits.org
- Gift of Adoption Fund, giftofadoption.org

- Katelyn's Fund, katelynsfund.org
- Adoption Airfare, Adoptionairfare.com 800-277-7651
- Both Hands, bothhands.org
- Lightstream loans, lightstream.com/

Book: You Can Adopt without Debt, by Julie Gumm

Birth Parent Support

Birth Mother podcasts:

- Birth Mothers Amplified (Muthoni and Emma)
- Birth Mother Matters in Adoption (Kelly Rourke-Scarry)
- Birth Moms Real Talk (D Yvonne Rivers)

Support Groups and Where to Find Them

- Online Support Groups such as Facebook are the easiest to find and the quickest to join.
- BraveLove.org has some events honoring birth parents.
- Most adoption agencies will have their own small communities of birth parents.
- https://www.birthmotherassistance.com/ search online by state. Not all are up to date.

Other Adoption Resources

Adoption podcasts:

- The Infant Adoption Guide Podcast (Tim Elder)
- Adoption Now (April Fallon)
- The Adoption Connection, by and for adoptive parents (Lisa Quails & Melissa Corkum)
- The Forgotten Adoption Option podcast (Marcy Bursac)
- Creating a Family.
- The Adopting & Fostering Home, Thriving Adoptees (Simon Benn)
- The Pregnancy Help Podcast
- Life Has Purpose (Ryan & Bethany Bomberger)

Adoption Encouragement for Women facing Unplanned Pregnancy

- Brave Love www.bravelove.org/tags/being_a_birth_mom
- Unplanned Good www.unplannedgood.org/i-chose-adoption, I chose adoption for my baby – Unplanned Good

https://www.unplannedgood.org/all-stories

Free eBooks:
https://resources.care-net.org/free-resources/

ABORTION

Abortion Industry Workers

ATTWN. And Then There Were None abortionworker.com/ A nonprofit organization whose mission is, "We help people in the abortion industry leave their jobs and rediscover the peace and joy they've been missing." ATTWN provides encouragement and licensed counseling for abortion industry Quitters. They connect former workers with life-changing resources including financial assistance, legal representation, employment opportunities, emotional healing, spiritual support and educational scholarships. ATTWN has helped over 600 abortion industry workers and 7 full-time abortion providing doctors escape and heal from their jobs in 44 states. Find ATTWN (and their Annual Report) at abortionworker.com/

Abortion Pill Reversal

AbortionPillReversal.com 877.558.0333 The Abortion Pill Rescue Network provides free and confidential care 24/7. If you hope to reverse the effects of the first abortion pill (mifepristone), contact a doctor at the Abortion Pill Rescue Network **immediately.** There are 800+ medical providers trained in this process; find one near you now.

Post-Abortion

- Rachel's Vineyard https://www.rachelsvineyard.org/
- Not Forgotten Ministries https://theyarenotforgotten.com/

- Hurt After Abortion https://hurtafterabortion.com/
- Support after Abortion https://supportafterabortion.com/
- Hope Support Online - First & Third Thursday of every month via Zoom, 6:30 pm to 7:30 pm, PST. Email hope@realoptions.net for the Zoom Link.

Information about the various health consequences of abortion.

- **For more detailed information on Abortion and MENTAL HEALTH,** refer to https://aaplog.org/wp-content/uploads/2019/12/FINAL-Abortion-Mental-Health-PB7.pdf
- **For more detailed information on Abortion and PRETERM BIRTHS,** refer to AAPLOG's Practice Bulletin Number 5, November 2021: The Association between Surgical Abortion and Preterm Birth: An Overview https://aaplog.org/wp-content/uploads/2021/11/PB-5-Overview-of-Abortion-and-PTB.pdf
- And AAPLOG's Practice Bulletin Number 11, November 2021: A Detailed Examination of the Data on Surgical Abortion and Preterm Birth PG-11-A-Detailed-Examination-of-the-Data-on-Surgical-Abortion-and-Preterm-Birth.pdf (aaplog.org)
- **For more detailed information on Abortion and BREAST CANCER,** refer to Professional Ethics Committee of AAPLOG, Committee Opinion 8, January 5, 2020 Abortion & Breast Cancer https://aaplog.org/wp-content/uploads/2020/01/FINAL-CO-8-Abortion-Breast-Cancer-1.9.20.pdf

Disclaimer: Unplanned Good has listed this small subsection of resources for your convenience. We do not have first-hand experience with all of their service offerings and cannot guarantee their quality or professionalism.

ABOUT THE AUTHOR

Terri Marcroft is the adoptive mom of a young adult daughter who is the love of her life. Terri's all-time favorite action hero is her daughter's birth mother, who made an adoption plan while she was a senior in high school.

In 2008 Terri saw the need to talk more about adoption. Today less than 1% of young American women facing unplanned pregnancy choose adoption for their babies, yet there are about two million couples in the US hoping to adopt. After ten years of parenting and 25 in high tech marketing, she founded UnplannedGood.org in 2010. Terri leads the organization's efforts to encourage people to consider making an adoption plan when facing an unplanned, unwanted pregnancy. She lives in California but speaks all over the country to help others understand open adoption and how it works today.

Although choosing adoption is **very** difficult for any birth parent, it can also be beautiful and rewarding. Terri's work has led her to get to know a community of birth parents who share a bond and are proud to help others by telling their stories. Terri hopes to spread the word about open adoption as a healthy solution and a blessing to all in the adoption triad.

Learn more at www.unplannedgood.org/

Email her at unplannedgood@gmail.com

ACKNOWLEDGMENTS

With immeasurable gratitude for the many birth parents and adoptees who've given loving feedback and input, sharing their hearts and their stories with me along this journey, especially Ali W, Dominique W, John S, Laura B, Ricky, and Courtney.

With very special thanks to my writing partner, Kelly P, for her perspective, her insightful input, and her patience as she read and improved each and every chapter throughout the writing process.

And to my dear friends who read the book in draft form and gave me their astute wisdom:

Jodi J T, Valerie H, Dana C, Maria Z M, Jenny N, Ann S, Patty A, L M B, Katie M, Tim E, Ashley P, Richard H, Teri F, Buffie G, and Steve F.

And to my editors, Linda P and Tom G for their diligence and many corrections.

Thanks also to my family—Mom, Dad, Mike, and Janet—for their feedback and encouragement along the way.

If this book inspired you to advocate for adoption,
please go to Amazon.com and leave a brief review.

If you want to learn more about open adoption, read more testimonials
from the Triad, please visit unplannedgood.org/
If you'd like to help spread the word about open adoption, you can
donate to Unplanned Good at https://www.unplannedgood.org/donate

Made in United States
Troutdale, OR
01/27/2024

17194304R00086